I Feared Nothing:

The Autobiography of Qasem Soleimani, 1957-1979

Qasem Soleimani

Translated by Milad Mohammadi

Copyright © 2020 Lantern Publications

Original Persian Edition
Author: Qasem Soleimani
Title: *Az chizi nemitarsidam: zendegi-nameh-ye khodnevesht-e qāsem soleimāni, 1335 ta 1357*
Editor: Mohammad Mehdi Bagheri
Publisher: Tehran: Qasem Soleimani Library, 2021

All rights reserved. No part of this publication may be reproduced, distributed, or transmitted in any form or by any means, including photocopying, recording, or other electronic or mechanical methods, without the prior written permission of the publisher, except in the case of brief quotations embodied in critical reviews and certain other noncommercial uses permitted by copyright law. For permission requests, write to the publisher, addressed "Attention: - Permissions (Rihanna's Dream)," at the email address below.

Lantern Publications
info@lanternpublications.com
www.lanternpublications.com

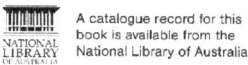

A catalogue record for this book is available from the National Library of Australia

Ordering Information:

Quantity sales. Special discounts are available on quantity purchases by corporations, associations, and others. For details, contact the distributor at the address below.

Shia Books Australia
www.shiabooks.com.au
info@shiabooks.com.au

ISBN- 978-1-922583-41-3

First Edition

In the Name of God,
the Most Compassionate, the Most Merciful

Prayers of God's Peace and Blessings

In keeping with the Islamic practice of showing respect for the name of God, and sending prayers of God's peace and blessings whenever the name of His blessed Prophet, Lady Fātema, and the Twelve Imams is mentioned, as well as for asking God to hasten the reappearance of the Lord of the Age on the Earthly plane, one or more of the following Arabic symbols have been employed throughout the text. They are repeated for their great rewards.

 Used exclusively after the name of God, meaning "the Sublimely Exalted", or, as a prayer, "[May His name be] Sublimely Exalted".

 Used exclusively after the name of the Prophet, meaning "May the peace and blessings of God be unto him and unto [the purified and inerrant members of] his family"

 Used for any of the Twelve Imams or past prophets of God , meaning "May God's peace be unto him".

 Used for Lady Fātema, meaning "May God's peace be unto her".

 Used for the Lord of the Age (the Twelfth Imam), meaning "May God hasten the advent of his noble person".

Translator's Preface

You are holding in your hands an English translation of the first ever book published by the Hajj Qasem Library. It is an autobiography of Qasem Soleimani, former commander of the Qods Force; an elite branch of Iran's Islamic Revolutionary Guard Corps (IRGC).[1] Of course, if you are reading this, then you are likely already familiar with this man and his life's work.

To be sure, this autobiography is an incomplete one. The author began writing the book late in his life and was assassinated before it could be completed. Thus, the book only covers his early life: his childhood in rural Kerman, his migration to the city as a teenager in search of work, and his involvement in the protest movement against the Pahlavi monarchy.

Soleimani is viewed primarily as a military leader, by his lovers and haters alike. However, this work is not a story of the life of *General* Qasem Soleimani – the commander, the strategist, and America's public enemy no. 1 – so much as it is an account of the exceedingly simple and modest lifestyle of rural (and more specifically, tribal) Iran prior to the Islamic Revolution in 1979.

---

[1] In Persian: *Sepāh-e pāsdārān-e enqelāb-e eslāmi.*

I Feared Nothing

What we see through the lens of Soleimani's early life is, in some ways, not too far removed from what the novelist Jalal Al-e Ahmad said of rural Iran: that 'half of its fifty thousand villages still do not know what a match is.'[2] Indeed, rural Iran was – by and large – a realm that had been untouched by time; regally indolent to the rapid changes that had been taking place in the world (and, indeed, within Iran itself).

Thus, this autobiography can be described as an origin story: a first-hand look into the humble beginnings of a man who would end up shaking the world to its core.

It may be beneficial to mention a few technical points about this translation. Transliteration of Persian words have been done according to the guidelines defined by the Association for Iranian Studies. Exceptions are made for the names of people and places, where instead the most prevalent English spellings are used (e.g. Kerman rather than *Kermān*).

The Persian language is not bereft of honorifics, and the author uses them on more than a few occasions in this book. English equivalents are used where possible; however, where it became necessary to use the original Persian honorifics, please refer to the footnotes for additional information.

The author writes in a stream of consciousness style. This style has been preserved as best as it could; however, some of the non-sequiturs (namely, those which do not translate well into English) have been ironed out in the interest of preserving the narrative flow.

As for the original manuscript, there were some challenges that the Hajj Qasem Library faced in transcribing and publishing it. The author's handwriting was unique, and thus the

---

[2] Jalal Al-e Ahmad, *Khārk: dorr-e yatim-e khalij* (Tehran: Amir Kabir, 1979): p. 12, as quoted and translated in Hamid Dabashi, *Theology of Discontent: The Ideological Foundation of the Islamic Revolution in Iran* (London: New York University Press, 1993): p. 59.

Translator's Preface

publisher enlisted the author's relatives to help identify certain letters and words. In spite of their best efforts, 25 words in the text were not identified with absolute certainty, and thus the publisher used their best estimation as to what these words were.

The parenthetical phrases you see throughout the book are all written by the author himself, with the only exception being those that contain translations of Persian words. The footnotes, however, are all by the translator, and mostly serve to offer contextual information that can hopefully serve to improve the reader's understanding.

In the interest of thoroughness, the original introduction to the book has also been translated. This introduction was written by none other than the author's daughter, Zeinab Soleimani, who – for all intents and purposes – has inherited her father's will.

Milad Mohammadi
25th of April, 2022

I Feared Nothing

Introduction

On the morning of Wednesday, the 16th of December 2020,[3] by the grace of God, I was granted the privilege of meeting with the Honourable Leader of the Revolution;[4] may my life be sacrificed for him. This was at a meeting between the leader, the Center for Commemorating Shahid Qasem Soleimani,[5] and us; Hajj Qasem's family members.[6]

---

[3] The Iranian calendar, also known as the *hejri-ye qamari* (Solar Hijri; hereby SH) calendar, is the primary calendar used in Iran. Whenever such dates are cited, I will convert them to their Gregorian equivalent while providing the SH date within the footnotes. The date cited above is equivalent to the 26th of Azar, 1399 SH.
[4] She is referring to Seyyed Ali Khamenei (b. 1939), the leader of the Islamic Republic of Iran, whose official title is *rahbar-e moazzam-e enqelāb-e eslāmi* (Honourable Leader of the Islamic Revolution).
[5] *Shahid* (martyr) is affixed before the name of a martyr, akin to a ceremonial title.
[6] *Hajj (or Haj)* is another title, which in terms of its lexical meaning, is meant to address a man who has completed his *hajj*; the Islamic pilgrimage to the holy cities of Makkah and Medina. However, in Iranian society, *Hajj* is often used more liberally; sometimes used to address any middle-aged (or older)

I Feared Nothing

Representing my father, I took a gift for the leader. This gift was Hajj Qasem's own autobiography, which I had intended to publish to mark the anniversary of his martyrdom.

What I had in my hands was, in fact, a rough draft of the book. At the end of the meeting, I gifted the text to *Āghā*.[7] He asked me some questions about it and then graciously accepted the gift.

Some days after that meeting, as work on the book was reaching its conclusion, I received a manuscript from the office of the leader. He had been hard at work writing his own memoirs in memory of his loyal soldier. This text was filled with a manner of benevolence and magnanimity; such that these characteristics were affixed to the book like a soul to its body.

I give thanks to the all-wise God, one thousand times over, for the existence of the leader. I remember that Hajj Qasem wrote the following, in his last will and testament:

'God, I am thankful to you that – after putting me at the service of your pure servant, my dearest Khomeini,[8] you placed me in the line of another pure servant; one whose oppressed-ness is even greater than his purity; the sagacious leader of Islam, Shi'ism, Iran, and the political Islamic world of today: my dearest Khamenei, may my life be sacrificed for his.'

Thus, some words about the work which you hold within your hands:

Writing this introduction is not an easy task for me. Girls know very well how difficult it is to bring into writing the infinite

---

man. In any case, Qasem Soleimani is often affectionately referred to as Hajj Qasem as opposed to his more formal title of *sardār* (general).

[7] Supporters of Seyyed Ali Khamenei sometimes affectionately refer to him as *Āghā* (mister).

[8] Seyyed Ruhollah Mousavi Khomeini (d. 1989), the most prominent leader of the Iranian revolution and the founder of the Islamic Republic of Iran.

Introduction

love that exists between father and daughter, let alone to do so as a preface to her father's book after he has been martyred.

My father was a martyr, even while he was among us. In a way, we all knew this. It was a truth that we learned to live with. Whenever I thought of the day when he would no longer be with us, stupor and anguish would come over my entire existence. This was the nightmare from which I would constantly flee.

Qasem Soleimani was organised and precise in his day-to-day life, as a military commander must be. He planned out every minute of his waking life. His long work hours and the sheer volume of his responsibilities often did not leave him much time to attend to personal affairs. However, there was one exception: studying and writing. Hajj Qasem considered reading to be an obligation, and imparted this upon us; his children.

His books of choice were across a broad spectrum of genres: from Persian poetry to foreign novels, to historical and political books, to memoirs and biographies, to military theory and history.

His manner of reading, likewise, was interesting in its own way: he would read a book attentively. As he would read, he would write notes throughout the book, within the margins of its pages. Sometimes, he would write more thorough notes within a separate notebook. He would often highlight the books with a marker. Thusly, he would become familiar with the books he read.

I Feared Nothing is an autobiography which Hajj Qasem wrote with his wounded hand. It is the account of the life of a man from a far-flung village in the heart of Kerman. Within its pages, he narrates the different stages of his simple life. This is the story of the emergence of a man who began as a shepherd and eventually reached a stature as high as the heavens.

Throughout the past year, many writers and researchers have attempted to commit to paper a biography of Hajj Qasem.

I Feared Nothing

All of these efforts came from respectful and sacred motivations. However, given that many chapters of his life were unknown,[9] these writers generally have insufficient or imprecise information. With this book, it is now possible to fill this void.

I would like very much that everyone who has only seen Hajj Qasem Soleimani in his officer's uniform to know how he was raised. *I Feared Nothing* is, thus, the starting point of a great mission: the mission of acquainting ourselves with a great man.

Zeinab Soleimani
November 2020[10]

---

[9] She is likely referring to certain events of Soleimani's life being unknown outside of the circle of his own family.
[10] Azar 1399 SH.

I Feared Nothing

My sister Hajar is very much learned about our tribe.[11] Her knowledge of our clan's lineage is unrivalled. According to our elders, our ancestor, the son of Ghorban, emigrated from Khorasan[12] along with his brother (who was, according to some, a blood brother, and according to others, among the elders of the

---

[11] The word the author uses here is *ashireh*, which can roughly be translated as tribe or clan. Other words which are colloquially synonymous – *tā'efeh*, *qabileh*, *khāndān*, *il*, *tabār*, and so on – will all, likewise, be translated as tribe or clan. The plural of *ashireh* is *ashā'er*; in Iran, *ashā'er* refers specifically to semi-nomadic peoples who migrate to the highlands during the warm seasons and to the lowlands during the cold seasons. The Soleimani clan are among the ethnically Lor clans of Kerman and likely emigrated from Khorasan to other regions of Iran before eventually settling in Kerman centuries ago.

[12] Khorasan refers to eastern Iran (in its historical definition, comprising much of central Asia). In contemporary times, it is typically only used in reference to the three provinces of current-day Iran which bear its name: North, South, and Razavi Khorasan.

I Feared Nothing

Fars region[13]). In the end, it is not clear whether this was due to them being exiled or for some other reason.

From Neyriz in Fars,[14] they trekked to the springheads of the river Halil. This river stretches from its source in the highlands – with elevations of between 3500 and 4000 metres – for over 300 kilometres before settling in Lake Jazmourian on the border between Kerman and Baluchestan provinces.[15]

Upon settling, they immediately took control over the lands surrounding the river to a radius of around 15-20 kilometres.

Mir-Ghorban[16] had four sons – named Vali, Mohammad, Hossein, and Ebrahim – and one daughter, who he married off to a man named Alidad. Over time, these four sons each form their own clan, and from their sons, yet even more clans are formed. Thus, the Soleimani tribe was formed from Mir-Ghorban's five clans; four from his sons, and one from his daughter, who today are called by surnames which attest to this: Mohammadi, Hosseini, Ebrahimi or Amir-Shekari, Mash Vali, and Alidadi.

My father and mother are from the two Zarali lines who are descended from Mash Vali. My father was from the Ebrahimi clan and his mother was from a Lori clan. Thus is my lineage.

For some reason, the Ebrahimis had more property than the others. However, over the course of time, my father sold some of these properties. Slowly, three classes emerged within the tribe,

---

[13] Fars is a province in southern Iran which borders Soleimani's native Kerman.

[14] Neyriz is a small city within a *shahrestān* (Iranian administrative division roughly equivalent to a county) of the same name, located in southeastern Fars province, close to Lake Bakhtegan. It is a historical city known for its pomegranates, sturdy knives, and many mineral deposits.

[15] Sistan-Baluchestan: Iran's southeasternmost province.

[16] Mir-Ghorban means 'the son of Ghorban'.

I Feared Nothing

the ruling class of which were the khans.[17] After the death of Mir-Ghorban, every khan was considered an elder of the Soleimani clan.

There was a person by the name of Gerami Khan, after whom came his sons: Mohammad Ali Khan, Hossein Khan, Seifollah Khan, Ahmad Khan, and Valiollah Khan. My father's ancestors were from the Ebrahimi line, Lashgar Khan, and so on. Because of my kinship and shared roots with the khans, I did not see any particular corruption from them during my lifetime. Generally, they were responsible for resolving disputes within the tribe and supporting tribe members, as well as managing the tribe's relationship with the state.

They had a great deal of property, and one of their best properties was in the hands of my father, who – owing to his and my mother's familial inheritance – owned a share of this property. My mother was the daughter of Asadollah, and both she and her mother Zahra were from the Zarali clan.

However, I should make mention of my maternal kinships: evidently, after the *khāstegāri* ceremony,[18] my mother married my father at the age of 14. Typically, in our tribe, the length of the *aqd* was two years.[19] In any case, they married each other.

Jahangir narrates: 'On your father's wedding day, he was riding a camel. The camel fled and escaped, with the groom in tow! Fortunately, after some time, they managed to retrieve the camel.'

---

[17] Khan refers to a regional military leader. I have not italicised the word as it is not uncommon to see it being used in English.
[18] *Khāstegāri* is the traditional Iranian marriage proposal.
[19] Iranian culture has a wide variety of marriage-related ceremonies; perhaps more so than most cultures. The *aqd* is when the married couple is declared married in the Islamic jurisprudential sense. This usually predates the main wedding ceremony by some time.

I Feared Nothing

In the early period of my parents' married life, my father was in a state of extreme poverty. However, gradually he came to own some livestock, to the extent that sometimes he even needed one or two shepherds to help him. The first fruition of their marriage was a girl, whom they named Sakineh. At the age of three, she passed away from a bacterial infection. Shortly thereafter, my sister Hajar and my brother Hossein were born, and after them, I was born in 1957.

One particularly cold winter, I succumbed to German measles.[20] My parents did not have any hope that I would recover. They used every medicine that was available to them in the region, but to no avail. My father recounted that, in the midst of knee-high snow, he tied me to my mother's back as they trekked to Rabor[21] to get a doctor to diagnose me. In any case, after being sick for some time, the will of God ❀ was such that I remained alive.

My affection towards my mother – and perhaps her reciprocal affection towards me – caused her to nurse me for three years as opposed to two. Being separated from the kind bosom of my mother was difficult, but I slowly adapted.

Gradually, I was transferred from my mother's lap to being carried on her back, under her *chādor*.[22] Sometimes, from morning till noon, I would be riding her back under her closed *chādor*. And for this entire time, she would be busy with work. She would be harvesting, collecting sheafs, sweeping the home, milking the goats, baking bread, or cooking food.

---

[20] German measles (or rubella) is an infectious virus whose symptoms are light fever and red skin rash.

[21] Rabor (or Rahbor) is a mountain town situated roughly 175 kilometres from Kerman (city), 35 kilometres from Baft, and seven kilometres from Qanat-e Malek.

[22] *Chādor* – which literally translates to 'tent' – is a type of cloak worn by women in Iran.

I Feared Nothing

And what a tranquility I would feel while being with her! I would even fall asleep in that position. I feel that my mother, likewise, felt peace with my warmth. As I started walking, I also began a life of work. I would follow my mother barefoot, or with rubber shoes which my mother would get from wandering merchants in exchange for fleece or cotton.[23]

Like a duckling, I would follow her. Throughout the day, I would fall to the ground multiple times, or have my hands and feet get caught on thorns. When blood would trickle from my toes, my mother would gradually pull the thorns from out of my feet with a sewing needle and apply ointment on the affected areas with *oshtorak*.[24]

I loved the arrival of spring. Our winters were extremely harsh. I would wear my nylon shirt – which we called a 'wash and wear' – without any undershirt or overshirt. Iran,[25] Keramat's wife, would sew it for me. Sometimes, the harshness of the cold would push us to either wrap ourselves in the bedsheets or in my mother's *chādor*.

My mother would firmly wrap her headscarf around my head so as to, in her own words, shield my ears from the wind. In the harsh cold, I was constantly grinding my teeth. In the winters, my mother would feed us dried foods which were as hard as rocks. Chewing just one turnip would take half the day. Sometimes, she would also give us some oleaster, torrified wheat, and nuts.

A winter pastime of mine and my siblings was to roast potatoes over a fire pit. The moment the sky would clear up, we

---

[23] By wandering merchants, the author is referring to intermediaries who would exchange the surplus products of tribes and villages for goods purchased from shopkeepers in cities.
[24] *Oshtorak* (also referred to as *voshā*) is a plant with medicinal and industrial uses. It is especially commonly found in Yazd and Kerman.
[25] Iran is a somewhat common female name in Iran.

would flee to Samad's home – which got a lot of sunlight – and warm ourselves there.

As we were growing up, our favorite winter games were snowball fighting and *kāgubāzi*.[26] Hossein Jalali would come from Zardloo[27] and play with us children. He would mercilessly hit us all! We were always waiting with anticipation for the arrival of spring, and to flee the harsh cold and hardships of winter.

Spring, for us, was a season of blessings; firstly, for serving as an escape from the bone-chilling cold of the winter, and secondly, for being our season of migration.[28] As soon as Norouz would come and go, our clan would migrate toward the hills of Tangal.[29] This was done after the 13th, as the women believed it to be an inauspicious date.[30] Tangal was a sparse forest with wild almonds that would bloom in spring, as well as a large orchard where various fruits were grown.

The deep, green valley was ripe with *bondar* walnuts.[31] The canopy of walnut trees would not let sun light touch the earth below them, and tens of fountainheads were flowing from the small valleys, forming small rivers. The tall willow trees and white poplars, with their heads pointing toward the heavens, would cast large shadows over the land.

---

[26] By *kāgubāzi*, the author is perhaps – in his regional accent – referring to *kabkbāzi*, a game of finding partridges (*kabk*) who hide in the snow.

[27] One of the villages of Hanza, in the Baft region of Kerman.

[28] As mentioned earlier, the Soleimanis were among the *ashā'er* (tribes) of Iran, who live a semi-nomadic lifestyle. The migration is referred to as *kooch* in Persian.

[29] Tangal, or Tangal-huni – six kilometres southeast of Rabor – is a region of heavy snowfall and lush flora.

[30] Norouz is the Iranian new year, observed on the vernal equinox of each year. *Sizdeh be dar* (literally 'throwing out the thirteenth') is among the many Norouz customs, and is marked on the 13th day after the new year. This is generally when Norouz festivities end.

[31] *Bondar*, in the Kermani accent, refers to the lush areas of a valley.

I Feared Nothing

My mother would place the tent fabric by a stream and affix them to poles.[32] The pattering and splashing sounds of the water – which would flow right through the middle of our tent – would give us a sense of tranquility, even if our poverty and hardships would not afford us the opportunity for truly appreciating this tranquility.

Spring was the season of milk and yoghurt; the season of the bleating of baby goats and lambs, and of ewes being milked. The women of the family, crammed together densely, would carry flasks full of milk and were careful that not even one drop of it spills to the ground.

They would give out jugs to those who were short on milk. This generally occurred in the beginning of summer when the goats' milk would dry up.

In those days, when I would ask my mother for yoghurt, she would say: 'No, son! Today is your aunt's turn,' or 'It's the turn of Iran, Mash Aziz's wife.' In the spring, to attend school, we (meaning myself, the Alikhani family's children, Taj-Ali, Ahmad, and Samad's kids) would walk from Mount Tangal to the winter village of Qanat-e Malek.

We would carry our lunches on our backs. Our lunch generally consisted of one or two pieces of bread, along with some nuts and sometimes cheese. Sometimes, date *kolu* [33] would also be packed for us. These were made from the dates that Ebrahim, my mother's cousin, would bring back from Garmsir in a *saft*

---

[32] The tent fabric the author is alluding to is referred to as *palās* or *siyāh-chādor*. They are woven from mohair and stood up using a wooden pole at their center along with some other wooden poles and ropes surrounding it.
[33] *Kolu* is how the people of the region refer to what elsewhere in the country is called *kolucheh*. It is a cake-like, cookie-sized confection with some kind of filling (typically made of dates or walnuts).

I Feared Nothing

(palm leaf basket).[34] We had grown so accustomed to simple, everyday joys and hardships that these became an inextricable part of our lives. And because we were always occupied with work, we felt neither the joys nor the hardships. It was as though both of these had become part and parcel of our existence.

In those days, there was no bath house. Instead, my mother would take a large copper pot, fill it with water, heat the water over a fire, and then adjust the water temperature using the water from the streams and wash us with laundry soap (or sometimes with *eshlum*).[35]

I owned two pairs of clothes and one patched-up pair of rubber shoes. My mother would periodically boil the clothes in hot water to kill off any fleas and lice. Then, she would wash the clothes by the stream and lay them out to dry. In those days, municipal workers would come and fumigate the homes. My mother would apply DDT to the clothes (which we now know was very dangerous),[36] in order to deal with fleas and lice.

My mother would always make a bit of *pest*,[37] enough to fill one *javāl*.[38] Sometimes, in the afternoons, she would make *pest* with a bit of meat. Later, when I moved to the city, my

---

[34] It is unclear where the author is referring to by Garmsir. There is a village by the name of Garmsir in Ardestan, Esfahan, but it is unlikely that the author is referring to this village, given its remoteness and distance from Rabor. What is more likely is that he is simply referring to the tribe's winter settlement, as *garmsir* means 'warm climate'.

[35] *Eshlum* (or *oshnān*) is a plant with multiple uses: it can be used as animal feed, dye, and for various medicinal purposes. In addition to this, if you mix the ashes of a burnt *eshlum* plant with animal fat, the resulting product can serve as a natural soap.

[36] DDT (Dichlorodiphenyltrichloroethane) is a chemical compound originally developed as an insecticide. However, in recent decades, there has been a greater awareness of the harms that DDT poses to ecology and public health.

[37] *Pest* is a food made from wheat shoots and cracked barley. These are mixed with oil, spices, and water until the mix has a doughy texture.

[38] *Javāl* is a type of woolen handcrafted bag.

I Feared Nothing

mother packed some *pest* for me to take for the road. Whenever I would prepare and eat this food in the presence of city people, they would think it was dough! However, it was very delicious.

Nonetheless, in the harsh cold of winter, I was raised with not much clothes on my back.

Since I was a young child, I had a bit of a fearless streak. I recall one summer, when I was ten years old, school was out, and it was our harvesting season; we would harvest from sunrise till sunset. My father had a rather dangerous horned bull which everyone feared. He would have me ride on this bull to go to a village fifteen kilometres away where my aunt lived.

The prideful bull was not prepared to acquiesce to orders, and would constantly ram his head into my small legs. I traversed the desert, riding upon this dangerous animal, all the way until I reached my aunt's home.

One night, my father took me to where all the harvested wheat were stored, along the corollary of the river which was quite far from our home. That same night, a sounder of wild boars descended upon the wheat. My father and I climbed up a fig tree. My father made a big ruckus in an attempt to scare them off, but the prideful boars paid no heed. In the heart of the night, the sounder ruined much of the wheat. My father and I, atop the fig tree, were reduced to mere spectators.

Of course, it was not always so bad. Nonetheless, for all of winter – and into the second month of spring – our eyes were always fixed on the *javāl* of wheat; observing the wheat slowly but surely finish. My mother took great caution to prevent us from suffering hardships; thus, to supplement the wheat, she would mix in some green peas. Once or twice a week, she would use this to bake *arzan* bread,[39] a type of bread reserved only for the poorest of poor people.

---

[39] *Arzan* bread is a regional bread of the people in Rabor.

I Feared Nothing

Although we did not have much, not a day passed in which our home was bereft of guests. Two or three times a year, we would eat rice; which was colloquially referred to as *qabuli*.[40] No one would ever cook *āsh*[41] on their own; instead, the women of the clan – all of whom were cousins – would come together and cook a *nazri*[42] *āsh* to honor *seyyed-e khoshnām, pir-e khoshnām* (the noble sayyed, the noble elder),[43] to pray for rainfall, or to seek an auspicious seasonal migration. The *āsh* was quite delicious.

Some of the women of the family would also give a sugar lump (*kalleh qand*) as *nazri* and place it in the altar of the pilgrimage site, only for us kids to go take the sugar lump and eat it! Haji Rafi, whose lineage and family tree I am unaware of, had a small hamlet to himself. Once a year, on the day of Ashura,[44] he would make *halim*[45]; around three or four large pots' worth. From all the surrounding hamlets, people would flock to Haji's home – with a pot or a bowl in hand – to retrieve some *halim*.

---

[40] *Qabuli* rice is a type of steam-cooked rice which is served alongside peas or beans.

[41] *Āsh* is a type of Iranian soup made with greens, beans, and either noodles or barley.

[42] A *nazri* is a large amount of food intended to feed a large amount of people, prepared with some ritual intention (usually for honouring the deceased). One of the most common times of the year for *nazri* is during Shi'i mourning commemorations.

[43] There are a few graves of *imāmzādeh* (direct descendants of one of the twelve imams ﷺ) in the region, which are popular pilgrimage sites for the local people. It is unclear exactly which of these the author is referring to by *seyyed-e khoshnām, pir-e khoshnām*.

[44] Ashura (literally 'the tenth' in Arabic) is the 10th day of the Lunar Hijri month of Muharram, and the anniversary of the date of the slaying of Imam Husain ﷺ, the third imam of Twelver Shia Muslims. It is the most important mourning commemoration for Shia Muslims.

[45] *Halim* is a type of thick soup made from grains, legumes, and meat. It is commonly eaten (with regional differences) across south, central, and west Asia.

I Feared Nothing

My maternal grandfather, Haj Abdolkhaleq, travelled from here all the way to Makkah with just a horse and donkey. His journey took one full year. Some years, when hardships and hunger would make his life difficult, he would resort to eating wild greens.

Neighbouring us was a family which was utterly destitute. When my mother would bake bread, their children would stand and watch. The sight of seeing those two girls standing and gazing at the bread is still etched in my memory. My mother would give them some pieces of bread; this routine continued every day. Sometimes, my brother Hossein would get upset at them and reprimand them, but they were so hungry that they would not budge until they received the bread.

The school break, and my having received a passing grade of 13 on my report card, had no importance for me.[46] What I was focused on was the wooden branches which had been soaking in water.[47] In the morning, when I would see that a bunch of willow branches were resting inside the rain gutter, a quivering would come over my body.

One morning, the school principal picked me out of the queue.[48] He told me to show him the back of my hands. After I gave him my hands, he began hitting me with the soaked branches. My father heard the sounds of my cries, as the distance between the school and our home was a mere forty steps. He

---

[46] In the Iranian school system, grades are given on a scale of 20 (with 20 being the best possible grade). A passing grade is 10 and above.

[47] As will become evident from contextual information in the paragraph that will follow, these soaked branches were used by school personnel to beat the children. In those days, corporal punishment was quite common in Iranian schools.

[48] In Iranian schools, children queue in front of the school house every morning before reporting to their respective classrooms.

I Feared Nothing

called out: 'Mr Principal, why do you hit him? His skin is black.[49] He will not become white no matter how much you hit him!'[50]

In those days, boys and girls went to the same school.[51] I would go to the same school as my sister Azar and my brother Hossein. When the teacher would hit us, my sister – who was very brave – would attack the teacher with a small stick, cursing him through tears, crying out: 'Why do you hit my brother?!?'

Times were tough. We had some particularly cold and snowy winters. My father had gotten me a pair of rubber boots for the winter weather. However, the snowfall was well above my waist, and thus, the boots did not offer much in the way of relief. In fact, because the boots were made of rubber, they would make it feel even colder! One day, Bahram Faraji, who would come from Gonjan,[52] succumbed to frostbite and was brought to school unconscious.

The school's heater, much like my mother's oven, would invite us all to gather around it. We felt as though we wanted to hold the fire of the furnace in our embrace. The cold, the principal's mercilessness in giving us beatings, and our hunger, all went hand-in-hand.

The teacher, who was sent from the Literacy Corps,[53] had to be a jack of all trades. The Literacy Corps folks had a lot

---

[49] In Iran, people with darker skin are colloquially referred to as black. This is not to be confused with the Afro-Iranian community of Iran's southern coast, who are actually of African descent.

[50] Corporal punishment was given for a myriad of reasons, one of them being a child's presumed bad hygienic habits. The principal likely thought that the author was dark due to being unbathed rather than due to his natural skin tone.

[51] Under the Islamic Republic, from primary school until the end of high school, boys and girls attend school separately.

[52] Gonjan is a village nine kilometres from Rabor.

[53] The Literacy Corps (*sepāh-e dānesh*) was a volunteer organisation modelled after the Peace Corps in the United States. High school graduates who joined

of power. Sometimes, they even acted as the local police force. Every year, we would get a new teacher. The best among them was Tashakori, the first teacher from my first year of primary school. He was very kind.

It was in those days that handing out biscuits to the students started to become common practice. When the cartons of Georgian biscuits were unloaded, the resulting scent was sweeter than anything in the world![54] How pleasant it was when the principal would distribute the biscuits during our break time.[55] This was the first time in my life that I had eaten biscuits, and to this day, I still crave to experience a flavour so sweet.

The principal would typically be hosted by one of the locals every night, and we school students were charged with cleaning and sweeping his room. The principal had an intimidating aura to him.

It was a good year. The weather had become sufficiently spring-like. The thickets were all green and surrounded by green grass and flowers. The ewes got their fill, and the male goats would chase after the females. The sound of the bell made them drunk with happiness.[56] Clear water was flowing from the valleys, shining like silver.

The sky was pitch dark. We moved toward our tents. In the dark of the night, my feet were flapping around in my rubber shoes, which were torn and which I had patched four times with a hot iron. My toes became battered and bloody from hitting

---

the organisation, upon completing four months of military training, were sent for two years to teach literacy to residents of villages and far-flung cities.

[54] Georgian biscuits (*biskevit-e gorji*) was/is a brand of biscuits, unrelated to the country of Georgia.

[55] In Iranian schools, the break period (*zang-e tafrih*) occurs between each class period.

[56] The author is referring to the goat bells used by herders to take their goats out to graze.

against the rocks. Not a single day passed where thorns would not get caught in my feet. Every day, I would use a needle to remove the thorns. And of course, socks were nowhere to be found. Every year, I went through two pairs of these plastic shoes, which I would purchase by means of *pāchini*.[57] My shirts, as I mentioned earlier, were 'wash and wear' shirts, which my aunt Kobra or Iran would sew for me.

The weather was quite cool, and – wearing only a ragged old shirt – I felt a chill in my feeble body. The stark black valley was filled with the echoes of the singing of us kids, who were ten or eleven years old at the time. My *kordi* singing was better than all of theirs, if I may say so myself.[58]

The ewes, on instinct, knew the way home quite well, and boisterously moved toward their destination. That year, a leopard had been spotted in the valley, and likewise there were rumours of bears being spotted in the walnut trees. Thus, the extra noise we were making was mostly for the sake of scaring off any wild animals, as well as being a means of calming ourselves.

From a distance, I heard the sound of the village men calling out. Haj Azizollah, more so than everyone else, had been worried and came to welcome us back. He had with him a small axe, which, in a fight, could have made easy work of any adversary. Lovingly, he told us: 'Kids, you are late. We were very worried.'

The light of the oil lamps in the tents were visible, albeit vaguely. The goats instinctively dispersed and quickly flooded into their respective owners' homes. The sounds of their bleating

---

[57] When one shakes a walnut tree to gather its walnuts, some may remain hidden from sight. *Pāchini* refers to the act of gathering these hidden walnuts as well as extracting the syrup from the trees. The author would do *pāchini* and then barter the product for shoes.

[58] By *kordi*, the author may be referring to a type of singing whereby four verses of poetry are recited in song form.

brought about a beautiful ambience. In this sequence, I saw the power of God ﷻ. I saw how much understanding – in accordance with their natural needs – God ﷻ had given to these otherwise unassuming animals, to the extent that even in pitch darkness, they are able to recognise their owners' homes.

My older brother Hossein, who fancied himself to be the elder of the house, and whose seniority generally manifested itself in forceful commands and prohibitions, quickly counted the goats to make sure we had not missed anything in the dark. This head count was not performed by counting the animals, but rather by identifying each of them based on the names we had given them. One by one, my brother identified each of them: 'Blondie', 'Ant', 'Black-head', etc.

My mother's black copper pot was beside the fire, and it appeared that food had been prepared. Its agreeable aroma roused my sense of smell, and from this alone I recognised the food: *adas polo*.[59] My mother's *adas polo* had no equal! We would only eat rice a few times in the year, but as luck would have it, only when we had guests.

Seyyed Mohammad had come to visit us.[60] Seyyed would recite lamentations,[61] and stayed in our home for three or four months out of the year. The best foods were saved for him. My father and mother respected him greatly, and thus, with his arrival, we would get our fill. Seyyed Mohammad was a close friend of my father, but after he lost his donkey, he would come to our home less often.

---

[59] *Adas polo* (lentil rice) is one of the national dishes of Iran. In its most basic form, it consists of lentils and rice, but it can also include fried onions, walnuts, raisins, and ground meat.

[60] Seyyed is the Persianised pronunciation of the Arabic word *sayyid*, which refers to someone descended from the Prophet Mohammad ﷺ.

[61] By lamentations (*rozeh*), the author is referring to the lamentations recited to honour the Prophet's ﷺ household (*ahlul-bayt*).

I Feared Nothing

In those days, I was not really aware; only later in life did I realise that within our large tribe, no one was as hospitable as my parents. Our home always had guests, even as the hungry eyes of myself and my siblings were constantly fixated on the *javāl* of flour.

My mother was very conscious of our flour levels. Sometimes, she would mix some barley flour and black seed flour into the wheat flour.[62] And when we did not have any guests, she would often bake *arzan* bread; perhaps once or twice a week. In those days, *arzan* and barley bread were the bread of the poor. Today, it is perhaps the opposite; *arzan* and barley bread, if they can even be found, are more expensive than wheat bread.

In any case, because of the serious belief in our household that 'the guest is beloved by God,' I do not remember my parents ever so much as frowning in the guests' presence. Most of our guests were strangers who would pass by our clan's area while enroute to other villages. They would ask for some tea, and my mother would serve them tea with cardamon and cloves. And yet, she would never give any to us! It was a sight to behold.

If the travelers happened to pass by at midday, my mother would also serve them lunch: usually bread and yoghurt, bread and *gureh-māst*, eggs, or *ābgarmu*.[63] If the guests were particularly important, my parents would slaughter a rooster for them and serve them chicken and rice.

I was a child when my grandmother passed away in our home. She was an extremely pious, beautiful, and lofty woman. I could hear the lamentations of my mother and my aunt Soghra from the neighbouring house. My uncle, who was a Quran

---

[62] In Kerman, there is a type of local flour made from *karv*, a type of black seed.

[63] *Gureh-māst* is a nutritious food made by mixing milk with yoghurt. *Ābgarmu* is the regional term for *eshkeneh*, a type of onion base soup which also contains eggs.

teacher, lived in Bagh-e Shah which was a stone's throw away from us.⁶⁴

My grandmother had just left this world. Our home was a room without any doors or windows. It was quite long, and thus – without any windows – it was also quite dark. The roofing consisted of wood and salsify, while the structure of the house itself was all adobe. From our house's singular room – which functioned as our kitchen, storage, bedroom, and living space – there was a gate to another area which was our hayloft. In the summer season, we would collect the hay and fleece so that we could feed this to the goats in the winter when there was no grass to pasture or if the goats could not go outside due to the snow.

There was a woman in our tribe named Hosniyeh. She was around 50 years old and had tuberculosis. Everyone had abandoned her, but my father carried her on his back and brought her to our house. My mother took care of Hosniyeh for four years, until she left this world. Not once did my mother or father ever make a drama about this.

In any case, my mother would fill my father's and Seyyed Mohammad's plates to capacity with rice. Seyyed would protest: 'Sister, why did you make our portions equal? He will eat all of it, but I am merely an old man.' Nonetheless, we ate our fill.

My father was a praying man. In those days, not many would pray *namāz*,⁶⁵ but my father had an extreme steadfastness to *namāz* even in those times. He would pray the morning (*fajr*) prayers based on the position of the stars and the noon (*zuhr*)

---

⁶⁴ Bagh-e Shah – which after the revolution was renamed Bagh-e Shariati (after the revolutionary intellectual Ali Shariati) – is another village in Rabor *shahrestān*.

⁶⁵ *Namāz* (*salāt* in Arabic) refers to the five daily ritual prayers performed by Muslims.

prayers based on the positions of the shadows. Of course, in those days, mistakes in recitation were rather common.[66]

Just as he was steadfast in prayer, he was very conscious of *halāl* and *harām*.[67] The people of the tribe all knew this about him very well. He had gone to Mashhad and was known as Mashti Hasan.[68] He would pay his *zakāt* on time, whether in the form of wheat, barley, or goats.[69]

The thing my father did which was uncommon in our tribe, was *ghusl*.[70] Even in the coldest winter weather, he would perform *ghusl* in the village *qanāt*.[71] I will never forget that he and my mother argued about this on two occasions.

Ramadan came. From childhood, we all had a special affection for Ramadan. In the early mornings (*sahar*), we would put the principal's big radio atop two pieces of wood behind school house and gather around to listen. The sound was loud enough to be heard in the next three villages over!

That year, Ramadan fell in summer, and our tribe set up their tents next to the stream in Tangal. The water would pass by our home. The pleasant sound of the water flowing in the night,

---

[66] *Namāz* involves the recitation of verses of the Quran in its original Arabic. For non-Arabic speakers, perfecting the recitation typically requires some degree of literacy.

[67] In Islamic jurisprudence, *halāl* denotes something which is permissible, and *harām*, impermissible.

[68] The city of Mashhad in Iran's Khorasan Razavi province is home to the grave and shrine of Imam Ali ibn Musa al-Ridha ﷺ, the eighth imam in Twelver Shia Islam. This site is the most important pilgrimage site in Iran. 'Mashti' is a colloquial title given to those who have taken this pilgrimage.

[69] *Zakāt* is an Islamic tax-in-kind whereby the payer gives 2.5 percent of their wealth to the poor. It is a religious obligation; however, it is not enforced legally.

[70] *Ghusl* is a ritual bath which is recommended or obligatory upon Muslims for certain occasions or in certain situations.

[71] A *qanāt* is a system – dating back to ancient Iran – for transporting water from aquifers or wells to the surface.

the crystalline sparkle of the water in the day, and the cool, pure air from the snow-filled springheads of Mt. Tangal was enough to brighten anyone's soul.

During Ramadan, my father would say firmly to my mother: 'You have no right to feed those who are not fasting,' and my mother would give her typical response: 'Hasan, I cannot refuse food to a guest.' One time, he recommended to my mother that she not associate with people who did not pray. These discussions of my parents, and their attention to these issues, made me interested in religion; even without knowing anything about religion and its principles and its practical laws and commandments.[72]

My brother Hossein had pictures of footballers and singers which he had stuck up on the adobe walls within the dark corners of our house. One day, my father ripped them all up, saying they were in the way of the *qiblah*.[73] My brother was upset and got a good thrashing for it!

Much importance was given to pilgrimages and *imāmzādeh*s, as well as to the preparation of *nazri āsh*, the most important of which was for seeking rainfall. In our tribe, it was customary to offer the first goat from which a male kid was born, as *nazri* to Imam Husain ﷺ. They would keep it indoors for four to five months and feed it grass until it became the fattest of all the goats. Later, during migration season (which coincided with the start of autumn), they would recite lamentations for Imam Husain ﷺ, slaughter the goat, and serve a robust mutton dinner.

These rites were performed by poor and rich alike; by both the shepherd and the rancher. Seyyed Mehdi, the reciter, would go from home to home for one full month and recite

---

[72] In Twelver Shia Islam, principles (*usul*) refer to the essential beliefs of the religion, while minutiae (*furu'*) refers to its practical laws and commandments.
[73] *Qiblah* refers to the direction of the Kaaba in Makkah, to which Muslims face during their daily ritual prayers.

lamentations day and night. He would also accept people's payments, which consisted of a mutton chop as well as anywhere from two to five tomans.[74] The days of mourning were our best days. We would eat our fill. During the ceremony, the elders would sit on the higher ground, and we children on the lower ground.

Tea would be served. However, as per my father's recommendations, me and my siblings were not permitted to consume anything addictive. Thus, tea and cigarettes were both prohibited. In its stead, we would grab sugar cubes – which are, indeed, the pillar of tea – and eat them on their own. Later, when I went to the home of one of our kin for work, his teapot was sitting over the flame. The fragrance of tea and cloves spread through the air. He asked: 'You want some tea, son?' I answered in the affirmative. I had three large cups of tea with quite a bit of sugar. The flavour of this tea is still fresh in my memory.

On Thursday nights, I would recite the story of *moshkel-goshā* for my family as well as for our neighbours.[75] After the story was finished, some would bring raisin *nokhodchi*,[76] while others, who were not as well-off, would bring their *mafreshu*,[77] filled with sugar cubes. We would fill our pockets with these sugar cubes, which we enjoyed chewing on.

Summer was approaching its end, and the families were all preparing to pack up and return to the adobe domes of our

---

[74] Toman is the super-unit of the official Iranian currency, the rial. In those days, five tomans would have been roughly equivalent to eighty or ninety US cents.

[75] The story of *moshkel-goshā* ('remover of obstacles') is an Iranian spiritual folk tale. It is also part of a type of *nazr*, wherein after a particular problem is resolved, people gather together to eat mixed nuts (*ājil*).

[76] *Nokhodchi* is a type of traditional Iranian confection made from chickpeas.

[77] *Mafreshu* or *mafshu* is a type of regional hand-woven fabric pouch. They are used as a receptacle for small items, such as medicines, mixed nuts, chocolates, or, more recently, mobile phones.

I Feared Nothing

winter village. Thus, everyone would recite lamentations, one after another.[78]

My mother would frequently get headaches. Sometimes, she would faint from their severity. Me and my sisters would sit by my mother's bedside and cry. I was always worried about losing my mother. Any time my mother got headaches, my entire body would shiver. But this time, my mother's state was worse than usual. She was talking with my father discreetly, but I overheard her say: 'God is magnanimous.'

My father, in spite of having a feeble physique, was very strong mentally and had no fears. One day, his fearlessness got him into trouble: when Habibollah Khan, the tribal chieftain (*kadkhodā*), came to our hamlet. That day, it had snowed, and the local men all sat in the sunlight and talked with one another while we kids played in the snow. Habibollah Khan gave every man of the hamlet – except for Morid Mohammad, who in those days was a user – one small pipe of opium.[79] My father laughed and recited this poem: 'The generosity of the statesmen will bring the nation to the point where it is not needed.'[80] The chieftain became upset and had some harsh words for my father.

My elder brother became informed of the source of my mother's worries: my father's loan from the village's co-op bank.

---

[78] As mentioned earlier, the tribe would recite lamentations during their migration period.

[79] One of the expressions of hospitality among the people of those days – especially among villagers and tribal peoples – was to offer a small bit of natural opium in special gatherings. Prior to the revolution, opium was legal in Iran, and even – at times – rationed by the state; save for a period of crackdown on its cultivation from 1955-1969. Legal or not, the limited use of opium was considered socially and culturally acceptable.

[80] This proverb means something to the effect of: God 🕊 puts the leaders of a country in positions wherein they are ill-suited.

I Feared Nothing

My father was, as it turned out, 900 tomans in debt.[81] For this reason, he frequently visited the tribal chief's house to seek a resolution. My father's debt made me even more worried about my mother. I cried many times out of fear that my father would be imprisoned.

Ultimately, my brother Hossein decided to go to the city to find work and make some money to give towards my father's loan. He was sent off with a chorus of my mother's tears. After two weeks, he returned. He had been unable find any work. Now, my fears multiplied. At that point, I decided that I must go to the city by any means necessary, in order to pay off my father's debt. However, my father and mother were both opposed. I had just entered my 14th year.[82] I was a mere child, and a weak child who had not seen the world outside of Rabor, at that.

I insisted, nonetheless, and made an arrangement with Ahmad and Taj-Ali, who were like brothers to me.[83] We departed for the city on Mehdipour's bus, having with us a blanket, some bread wrapped in a cloth, and five tomans in cash. My mother made me go along with one of our relatives, as well, and gave him instructions on how to deal with me.

The bus arrived in the city of Kerman at night.[84] It was the first time I had ever seen such small cars. I was immersed in watching the cars drive past, when suddenly the bus stopped at Bagh Square. We waited for everyone to get off the bus, and then

---

[81] In those days, 900 tomans would have been equivalent to roughly 120 US dollars.

[82] In Iranian culture, age is sometimes expressed in terms of which year you have 'entered' as opposed to how many years you have completed. In this case, the author had entered his 14th year and was therefore 13 years old.

[83] Ahmad Soleimani (d. 1984) and Taj-Ali Soleimani (d. 1981) were cousins of the author. Both lost their lives in the Iran-Iraq war, which in Iran is referred to as 'the Imposed War' (*jang-e tahmili*) or 'the Sacred Defence' (*defā'-e moqaddas*).

[84] Kerman (city) is the capital of Kerman province, as well as its largest city.

I Feared Nothing

got off ourselves. Together, in the square, we laid out our blanket and opened our cloths that were filled with bread, nuts, and cheese. We were awestruck as we watched the passersby; it was like we were savages who had just seen civilised people for the first time!

We sat in a corner of the square. We were rather frightened when passersby would gaze at us. The question now was: where to go? We knew that we had to get to Abdollah's house, but none of us three knew how to hail a taxi, nor did we know the address. But Norouz (who my mother had sent to come along with us) had come to the city a few times before and was more experienced. He stopped a small orange car (which we later learned was called a taxi) and told the driver: 'To the end of Khaju Street, please.'

We rode the taxi and were on our way to Khaju. In just a few minutes, we were already on the outskirts of Kerman. When we got out of the taxi, we followed Norouz; trusting in his knowledge of the location of Abdollah's house. It was with great difficulty that I was able to carry my backpack as we walked. Nonetheless, we reached Abdollah's house. Three or four of our *ham-shahri*s were there, as well.[85] Abdollah gave us a proper welcome. I became elated at seeing him. I felt the fragrance of my *ham-shahri*s, of my mother, of my relatives, and of our village, and snapped out of my homesickness.

Ahmad began working in the home of an engineer, but everyone was convinced that no one would ever give me or Taj-Ali a job. That night, we got our fill of bread and yoghurt, and the next morning we began searching for work. Alijan, who moved to the city before us, was a good guide. I went to every shop, café, restaurant, and workshop I could find and asked: 'Do

---

[85] *Ham-shahri* refers to someone who hails from the same village, town, city, or region as oneself.

you need workers?' They would all take one look at my short stature and my feeble, skinny frame before declining.

Finally, I entered a building that was still under construction. Therein, some clever youths – black-skinned like myself – were hard at work. One of them was making cement in a cement-mixing tray. Another was carrying the cement across the worksite. Another was doing the same with bricks. One of them called out: '*Ustā!*'[86] *Ostād* Ali, who the boys called '*Ustā* Ali', took a look at me and asked: 'What's your name?'
'Qasem.'
'How old are you?'
'13 years.'
'Shouldn't you be in school?'
'I quit school.'
'Why?'
'My father is in debt.'

My eyes became filled with tears as the image of my father being handcuffed flashed before me. The tears began flowing down my cheeks, and I felt the absence of my mother. I exclaimed: 'Sir, I beg of you, give me work!' *Ustā*, feeling pity, asked if I can move bricks. I responded in the affirmative. He said: 'If you work, I will pay you two tomans per day.'[87]

I was happy that I found work. *Ustā* said: 'Come tomorrow at seven o'clock.' I asked: 'Tomorrow?' Then, I remembered that city people say tomorrow (*fardā*) instead of morning (*sobh*). I said: 'Yes, sir.' Happy, I made my way back to Abdollah's house – the sanctuary of my fellow travelers – and informed every one of my finding a job.

---

[86] *Ustā* is a colloquial way of saying *ostād* (which can mean professor, boss, or master).

[87] Two tomans would have been worth roughly 25-30 US cents at the time.

I Feared Nothing

In the morning, I went on my way. I arrived a half hour before when *ustā* had told me to come. No one was there. After twenty minutes, one of *ustā*'s apprentices arrived, and eventually, *ustā* himself appeared. I began moving the bricks from the pavement to the worksite. My small hands were nearly incapable of carrying even a single brick! Nonetheless, I continued working at whatever cost. As sunset approached, *ustā* gave me two tomans and told me to come again the next morning.

For the next six days, from sunrise until sunset, I was working at this worksite; a half-built building on Khaju Street. My feeble body and my young age did not lend me the capacity for such work. When carrying bricks, blood would drip from my small hands.[88] That afternoon, after work, *ustā* gave me twenty extra tomans and said: 'Here is your week's wage.'

Now I had around thirty tomans. With two rials, I bought a small package of Minoo biscuits,[89] and then I spent another five rials on some bananas. With these spoils, I had a good time, and somehow all of my fatigue was alleviated. In fact, this was the first time that I had ever eaten a banana. I even had to learn how to eat them from one of my workmates.

I reminisced about the day I walked with Ahmad from Rabor to our hamlet and saw that the teacher Hosseini-nasab was peeling the skin of an apple. As he and his friend walked, he threw the skins on the ground. Ahmad and I would pick up these discarded apple skins and eat them.

I can still taste the Georgian biscuits we were given at school. Even till today, nothing can quite match the sweetness of

---

[88] The coarseness of bricks can cause cuts on one's skin. It may be implied from the author's words that the other workers had developed thick skin and were able to carry the bricks without issue.
[89] Pars Minoo Industrial Company, established in the 1950s (and still around today), is perhaps best known for its biscuits and other snack products.

I Feared Nothing

those biscuits I had on that school day, in my hungry and youthful state.

On Friday, we went along with Taj-Ali, Alikhani, and Abdollah to the local *qanāt* to wash our clothes. My mother had packed for me a shirt and one toman in cash. The stream, whose crystalline water was irrigated to water a beautiful plain, reminded me of our beautiful village.

First, we went in the water and washed ourselves, using the laundry soap. Then we wore some clean clothes and washed our old clothes. My hands were too weak to scrub the clothes properly, but nonetheless, I managed to wash them. At night, in Abdollah's house, we had scrambled eggs with tomatoes. Abdollah was convinced that I could not continue my building job and that I should look for other work.

One day, I counted my money. I still had a long way to go to cover the 900 toman debt. I remembered my mother, my sisters, and my brothers, buried my head under the blanket, and cried. I fell asleep in a state of crying.

I awoke to the sound of the call to prayer (*azān*). I prayed ever since I was a child, albeit without knowing many of the correct etiquettes. I will always remember the sound of my father's prayer, and the supplication he would whisper after prostration:
'God, by Your Honour, do not debase me
For the crime of my sins, do not shame me
My shame is directed only to you
Do not make me ashamed towards any other'

I finished my prayer. I remembered our hamlet's pilgrimage to the noble sayyed and noble elder. I made a vow that if I managed to find a good job, I would leave a *kalleh qand* in his altar.

In the morning, we went along with Taj Ali and Abdollah; we went into every shop, café, kebab shop, and any open door we saw, asking if they needed any workers. They all took one glance at the both of us – looking weak and unkempt; like a pair of newborn calves yet to have even have a drink of milk – and said no. One kebab shop owner said he could hire only one of us, and was willing to pay four tomans per day.

Thus, Taj Ali was hired. It was difficult for me to separate from him in this city. We looked at each other and I began to shed tears. Abdollah tugged at my hand and we continued on our way. I kept looking back until we reached the end of the street. I did not want to forget the address of the kebab shop. Taj Ali, too, was weeping. He addressed me: 'Qasem, my friend', but I did not hear the rest of his sentence.

The job search started anew. For three days, from morning till night, I walked into every open door to seek work. I even lost track of some of the storefronts and asked for work multiple times.

I came across a street which had a number of hotels and travel lodges. One by one, I asked if they are hiring. At first, they would accept to hire me, but then after one hour they would rescind their offer. Eventually, I reached the end of the street. I entered a building and went up its stairway.

There was quite a bit of commotion. The aroma of food circulated in the air, and distracted me almost to the point of making me trip over. A middle-aged man was carrying trays of food and moving them about quickly. A chubby man was seated behind a table, counting a fistful of money. I was engrossed in watching him count the money as I became drunk from the smell of food.

The chubby man looked at me. A bit cross, he asked: 'What do you want?' I asked, with a voice of desperation: 'Sir, do you need any workers?' I was so desperate that I began to cry. The man's face changed. He said: 'Come here.' I went a few steps toward him. He looked at me with kindness and asked: 'What is your name?'

'Qasem.'

'And your surname?'

'Soleimani.'

'Don't you go to school?'

'Yes, sir, but I want to work, as well.'

The man called out for an '*Āghā* Mohammad'. A middle-aged man appeared, saying: 'Yes, boss?' The chubby man asked him to bring a plate of food. Some minutes later, he brought a platter of rice with *khoresht*.[90] It was my first time seeing such a dish. Later, I learned that this is called *chelo khoresht-e sabzi*.[91] 'Give it to the kid,' the boss said.

My tribal disposition – and the pride that my father and mother had inculcated in me – did not permit me to eat it at first. I said: 'No, thank you. I am full.' I said this, although I was so fatigued and hungry that I had not even the energy to move. The boss, who I later learned was called Haj Mohammad, said with much kindness: 'Come on, son. Please eat.' I ate the entire plate of food, and gulped down a whole bottle of Pepsi.

Haj Mohammad told me: 'You can work, sleep, and eat right here in the hotel. I will pay you five tomans per day, and if you are good, I will give you a raise.' My eyes lit up. I thanked God that my issue was resolved through the vow I had made earlier.

Haj Mohammad entrusted me to Mohammad, who was from Jiroft.[92] He took me into the kitchen. The chef was white-

---

[90] *Khoresht* can roughly be translated as stew. It comes in a variety of forms, and is usually eaten with rice.

[91] *Khoresht-e sabzi*, or alternatively, *qormeh sabzi*, is a *khoresht* made with greens, red kidney beans, and meat. The author was unfamiliar with the dish due to his simple and poor tribal upbringing.

[92] Jiroft is another *shahrestān* in Kerman province.

I Feared Nothing

skinned and rather plump. He gave me a nasty look. He said crossly to Mohammad: 'Where did you find this kid? This isn't child's play. I need a worker, not a child!'

My heart fell to my stomach. I imagined that all of my dreams were withering away. The white-skinned man, whose name was Yousefi, was arguing with Mohammad when a young man with a familiar accent interjected, asking: 'What's the matter, Mr Yousefi?' Yousefi, still cross, said: 'What is this that you've brought me?! He's not even as tall as the pots. How could he be of any help to me?'

The youth, coincidentally also named Qasem, asked me where I was from. I said Rabor. His eyes lit up. He asked: 'Rabor proper?' I answered: 'No. Qanat-e Malek.' Qasem laughed and said: 'I'm from Javaran.'[93] I wanted to cry tears of joy! Javaran is a village close to our tribal territory. My father would sometimes have business dealings with the shopkeepers there; trading mohair, wool, cotton, *kashk*,[94] and oil for other goods. He asked me who my father was. I replied: 'Mashti Hasan.' He knew my father well; it seemed my father was quite famous in Javaran. Qasem then told Mr Yousefi: 'This lad is my *ham-shahri*.' Yousefi fell silent.

Qasem became my most important safety valve; supporting and caring for me. I moved my belongings from Abdollah's house to the Hotel Kasra and began my work there. Soon enough, six months had passed. I sorely missed my mother, my brothers, and my sisters. Mr Yazdan-panah[95] had a son-in-law who was a cleric. Every now and then, I would see him come by. For extra income, I bought a juicer and started making juice

---

[93] Javaran is a village with a rather agreeable climate, within Rabor *shahrestān* and twelve kilometres from Rabor city.

[94] *Kashk* is a dried dairy product made from drained yoghurt.

[95] Yazdan-panah is the surname of the author's boss, the aforementioned Haj Mohammad.

in the streets. On Fridays, I would gather with Ahmad, Taj-Ali, and Alikhani.

The passersby were surprised when seeing my young age. Some would insist on paying my school expenses. Once, two middle-aged women – donned in hijab – came by. In those days, it was not too common to see women wearing hijab. One of the women asked me: 'What is your name, son?' I answered: 'Qasem.' She said: 'Qasem, dear, why don't you come along with me so I help you finish your schooling?' She insisted, but I said: 'No, I am fine. I can study while working.'

One night, I slowly counted my money; I had many two-toman notes, two-rial coins, five-rial coins, and ten-*shāhi* coins.[96] Altogether, I had 1250 tomans! I was so happy that I felt like my soul left my body. After five months, I successfully sent one thousand tomans to my father. It was perhaps the greatest success and victory I had ever achieved. With this, I was finally able to pay off my father's debt.

Nine months passed since my arrival to the city. I was no longer the skinny black kid I once was. I now felt the virility of youth surging inside me. Taj-Ali and I bought suits for ourselves. Mine had a very nice beige colour. The clothes and shoes together costed no more than one hundred tomans. I also bought a nice red shirt for two tomans.

I missed my mother a lot. Over the course of these nine months, there were dozens of occasions where I would cry when I thought of her. Now, the four of us (myself, Ahmad, Taj-Ali, and Alikhan) bought tickets from the Auto-Taj Garage and rode Mehdipour's car toward our village. I brought with me a suitcase full of souvenirs I had bought for everyone back home.

---

[96] The *shāhi* is a unit of currency first used during the Qajar period. Unlike the rial and toman, there is no such unit of currency in Iran today.

I Feared Nothing

I was in quite the good mood. A heavy snow had fallen and dressed everything in white. I remembered days past when the snow was as high as the goats' stomachs; when I would venture into the forest of almond trees without any fear of the wolves who would use the snow as cover to hunt the goats; those days when my father would buy me rubber boots.

Near Bezanjan,[97] the car broke down. We walked a bit. On the way, we hitched a ride from a young chap in a jeep. Near sunset, we arrived. All the kids our age, and even the younger ones, came to receive us: Ahmad the son of Khodakaram, Gholam-Abbas, Ali Mohammadi, and so on. Our nice, colorful clothes and our refreshed appearance caused everyone to pour into town.

My mother and father were quite happy. My mother slaughtered a chicken and prepared a thorough dinner. I distributed the souvenirs to everyone. And naturally, I had brought something for each of my two sisters, who were very dear to me.

I also bought a Lubitel camera.[98] With it, I took some pictures with the local children. My father was very happy. Without delay, he asked about my work: 'Son, is your work hard?' 'Are your work mates treating you well?' I answered in the affirmative.

After ten days, we returned to Kerman. However, this trip was very different from the first one. I no longer feared the city. I no longer felt like a stranger in a strange land. The sight of cars was no longer strange to me.

---

[97] Bezanjan is a town in Kerman's Baft *shahrestān*. It is 151 kilometres from the provincial capital.

[98] Lubitel was the name of a line of cameras manufactured by the Soviet company LOMO (*Leningradskoye optiko-mekhanicheskoye obyedinenie*).

I Feared Nothing

After returning, I took up sport. First, I joined the Ataei *zurkhāneh*,[99] and later the Jahan *zurkhāneh*. May God 🌸 have mercy on Mr Ataei. When he was alive, he was there every evening. Although he had an athletic physique, he did not participate in the exercises himself due to issues with his leg. Everyone else at the *zurkhāneh* was older than me.

In the Jahan club, there was a strong athlete whom I would befriend after the revolution, named Abbas Zangi-abadi. He could do more than fifty reps of stone-lifting and a hundred reps of push-ups.[100] I had another comrade, named Ata, who was a taxi driver. If he grabbed your wrist, there was no escaping from it. The first karate class in Kerman was taught by the now dearly departed Mr Vaziri, and I was among those who signed up for it. Altogether, there were thirty of us in the class. I eventually managed to attain the rank of green belt.[101] In addition to martial sports, I did strength training and body building twice a week.

Gradually, I got into the idea of renting a home. Together with Ali Mohammadi and Ahmad, who by then had joined me in working at the hotel, we rented a room from an old lady named Asiyeh. The building was on what was then called

---

[99] The *zurkhāneh* (house of strength) is a traditional-style Iranian strength training and wrestling/grappling gym, best known for their coordinated strength training exercises supplemented by a special brand of *zurkhāneh* music. This assortment of exercises and training methods is referred to collectively as *varzesh-e bāstāni* (ancient sport), or alternatively, *varzesh-e pahlevāni* (strongman sport).

[100] The *zurkhāneh* stone (*sang*) is a heavy, flat, board-shaped stone with a gap in the middle where it is meant to be gripped. Athletes use these stones to do various upper body exercises. By push-up, the author is referring to what in English is called a divebomber push-up (or alternatively, a hindu push-up or judo push-up).

[101] The green belt constitutes the fourth and third *kyu* rank. After the green belt comes the brown belt (the second and first *kyu* ranks) and then the black belt (the *dan* ranks).

I Feared Nothing

Naseriyeh Street (which has since been renamed Shahid Bahonar Street).[102] Our rent was ten tomans per month.

Sport, and my faith in the values that had been entrusted to me by my mother and father, helped me to avoid going down a path of corruption; in spite of the corruption that was rampant in society. The words of Haj Mohammad and *Āghā* Seyyed Mojtaba,[103] likewise, had a big effect on me.

The first time I ever heard someone speak ill of the Shah was in 1974.[104] I was talking with Ali Yazdan-panah in the mess hall.[105] It was the 26th of October,[106] the Shah's birthday. I was reading a poem in the newspaper commemorating this occasion. I saw that this made him upset. He said: 'Don't you know that all of the corruption you see around you is because of this family?' I became upset and asked: 'Which corruption?' Ali spoke of the forced unveiling of women and the construction of centres for corruption.[107] His words left me speechless. In those days, the Shah was – in my mind – above reproach. Him speaking these words were as if he had taken a sledgehammer to my entire worldview!

---

[102] Named after Mohammad Javad Bahonar, the revolutionary cleric who briefly served as prime minister of Iran before being assassinated – along with other government officials – by the People's Mujahedin (*Mojāhedin-e khalq*, or MEK for short).

[103] It is unclear who the author is referring to by Seyyed Mojtaba, as this is the first and only time in the book that he refers to such a name.

[104] The author is referring to Mohammad Reza Pahlavi, then ruler of Iran.

[105] Ali was the son of the author's boss, Mohammad Yazdan-panah.

[106] 4th of Aban, 1353 SH.

[107] The forced unveiling of women (*kashf-e hejāb*) occurred under Reza Shah (father and predecessor of Mohammad Reza Shah), but the Pahlavi dynasty in general was inclined towards undermining traditional expressions of religiosity (hijab being chief among them), and pursued this policy through a myriad of means. 'Centres for corruption' (*marākez-e fesād*) refers to gambling dens, brothels, and the like.

I Feared Nothing

Ali had chosen his path and was resolute in having done so, but for a few days, I was in a state of confusion. I had faith in Haj Mohammad, who was a pious man. Thus, I went to him and told him what his son had told me. He brought his hand up to his face and said, harshly: 'Shhh! Shhh!' His reaction frightened and surprised me. I looked around, but no one was there. He tried to tell me, this time in a more gentle tone, to forget about what Ali had said.

The next day, Haji called me in and asked: 'You didn't tell anyone anything, did you?' I said no. He gave me ten tomans as a reward. I said: 'But I wanted to know if what Ali said was true. Is it true that the Shah is behind all the corruption?' Haj Mohammad took a glance at his surroundings and said: 'Man, you really need to watch what you say! SAVAK will give you a rude awakening.'[108] With prideful indolence, I asked: 'Who is Savak?' Haj Mohammad shushed me once again.

I realised that Haj Mohammad was not going to tell me anything, so I started fraternising with Ali more frequently. Without a care in the world, he started to speak of things which, at the time, were unbelievable for me: about the Shah, his wife, his sisters, and so on. Ali Yazdan-panah, Haji's son – who was a bit on the chubby side – spoke words that subjected my worldview to a serious internal conflict.

I thought about this long and hard. One night, I spoke with Ahmad. Bahram Faraji, whose father was my father's cousin, was also there. I noticed that Bahram said some things that were similar to what Ali Yazdan-panah had told me before; not of the Shah's corruption, but of his tyranny: that he was

---

[108] *Sāzmān-e etelā'āt va amniyat-e keshvar* (National Intelligence and Security Organisation), or SAVAK, was the secret police and intelligence service of the Iranian state under the Pahlavi dynasty. They were notorious for their violent crackdown of opposition movements and their torture of revolutionary activists.

I Feared Nothing

imprisoning and killing people. He also mentioned that the Shah suppresses the mourning ceremonies for Imam Husain ﷺ.

Impulsively, I – who was raised with these mourning ceremonies since childhood and looked forward to the recitations of lamentations all year long[109] – said loudly: 'He does what?! To hell with him!' Bahram suddenly became as pale as gatch.[110] Taken aback, he said: 'Are you trying to get us nicked?!'

The year was 1975/76.[111] Ahmad and I, to further help out our fathers, brought two of our brothers – Sohrab and Mahmoud, who were around the same age as one another – to the city with us. Now there were five of us in the room; which served as a bedroom, kitchen, storage facility, and everything else. The landlady, Asiyeh-*khānum*, had no one. Thus, we would give her some of our food. However, Ahmad paid more care to the old lady than I did.

Next door to us lived another poor old lady, named Masoumeh, along with her orphan child.[112] Ahmad would give her child (who was named Mehdi) lessons. Indeed, Mehdi was always a guest at our *sofreh*.[113] At nights, when we would gather, we would wrestle each other. Ahmad and I were the same age and at the same level of strength. Some nights, these grappling sessions would continue until midnight, but they never escalated into fights.

---

[109] The author actually writes 'from the new year until Mehregan'. Like many Iranian cultural festivals, Mehregan is based on the coming of a new season (autumn).
[110] Gatch is a type of white plaster commonly used in Iranian architecture.
[111] 1354 SH.
[112] In Iranian culture, children who have lost their father are often referred to as orphans, even if their mother is still alive.
[113] A *sofreh* is a cloth spread out on the floor during meal times. It is the functional equivalent of a dining table.

I Feared Nothing

It was the year 1976/77.[114] Following Ahmad's suggestion, I began attending the Qa'em Mosque,[115] wherein Mr Haqiqi[116] taught the recitation, meaning, and exegesis of Quran. From the Qa'em Mosque, I eventually found my way into the Fatemiyeh *tekiyeh*.[117] I would partake in most of their *ziyārat āshurā* sessions – with its one hundred curses and one hundred salutations – which were recited by Ata Khan.[118]

In those years, a cleric named Mahmoudi would give sermons at the Imam Mosque, which at the time was known as the Malek Mosque.[119] A large swathe of the masses would come and listen to him speak. He spoke in a pleasant and engaging manner. For everything he said, he provided a citation: this chapter, that verse, etc. I was heavily influenced by his speeches. Gradually, I began to develop a sense of religious spirit and zeal.

In the summer of 1976, the 'Garden Party' came to Kerman.[120] It is worth noting that the Shah had established centres for corruption in most all of the provincial capitals, aimed at misguiding the youth. However, in Kerman, his efforts were

---

[114] 1355 SH.

[115] The Qa'em Mosque of Kerman, located on Motahhari Street.

[116] Ayatollah Abbas Haqiqi (d. 2008) was a seminary teacher, exegete of Quran, and the imam of the Qa'em Mosque as well as Kerman's Jameh Mosque.

[117] A *tekiyeh* is a place for performing religious ceremonies, usually mourning ceremonies.

[118] *Ziyārat āshurā* is a salutatory prayer, often recited during mourning ceremonies for Imam Husain ؑ. The 'salutations' and 'curses' within this prayer are directed toward Imam Husain ؑ and his companions, and their killers, respectively.

[119] The Malek Mosque, or Imam Mosque, dates back to around a thousand years and has an area of around ten thousand metres squared.

[120] 'Garden Parties' were state-sponsored festivals held in parks or other large public spaces. They included performances by famous entertainers, and were usually held to mark some occasion of national importance or political importance to the monarchy.

I Feared Nothing

not quite as successful. At this Garden Party, however, all the famous singers and dancers – Aghasi,[121] Homeyra,[122] Hayedeh,[123] Azita, and the like – were brought to an open area at the end of Abu Hamed Street, which in those days was called Samsam Street.[124] They had set up a large tent. People flocked there to watch the singers and dancers perform.

Along with my friend Fath-Ali (the one from Javaran) and Ali Yazdan-panah, we decided to sabotage the event. At night, while everyone was busy watching the Garden Party performances, we pulled out 150 valves from the wheels of cars and motorcycles. Their tyres all went flat, and we escaped without a trace! In those youthful days, we combatted the corruption of the state like so; with pride and without fearing anyone. Of course, at the time, we truly knew nothing of SAVAK. I had merely heard of them through Haj Mohammad, who spoke of them with a sense of trepidation…but I feared nothing.

My friend Hasan had a Honda CB750 motorcycle. That summer, I would hitch rides with him as he rode like a madman through the streets. The pridefulness of youth, along with karate skills and a bit of muscle mass, gave me a bit of a propensity toward fighting and arguing.

I had already left the hotel job by 1974/75.[125] I was looking to work in a more specialised field. I became acquainted with two ceramic workers from Nazi-abad in Tehran.[126] They were very religious and very much opposed to the Shah.

---

[121] Singer-songwriter Nematollah Aghasi (d. 2005).
[122] Singer Parvaneh Amir-afshari, better known by her stage name Homeyra.
[123] Singer Masoumeh Dadehbala (d. 1990), better known by her stage name Hayedeh.
[124] Samsam Street is currently called Palestine Street.
[125] 1353 SH.
[126] Nazi-abad is a working class neighbourhood in southern Tehran.

I Feared Nothing

They insisted that I work with them. After working with them for six months, I came to learn that they were members of the *Mojāhedin-e khalq* (MEK) organisation.[127] They insisted on taking me back to Tehran with them, and their good manners left a big impression on me.[128] However, I succumbed to brucellosis and was unable to take them up on their offer.[129] Instead, I spent two weeks at the Raziyeh Firouz hospital receiving treatment.[130] By the time I was discharged, they had already returned to Tehran.

After my hospital stay ended, I managed to get a job with the help of an individual named Shafi'i, who was the water resource manager of Kerman province. Thus, I began my work as a meter reader for the provincial water company.

It was now 1976/77.[131] I would consistently be coming and going from the Jameh Mosque,[132] whose communal prayers were led by Ayatollah Salehi.[133] I continued to attend the Qa'em

---

[127] *Mojāhedin-e khalq* (MEK), or 'The People's Mujahedin' – founded in 1965 – was one of the many groups involved in revolutionary activities in the 1960s and 1970s. The group would later become notorious among Iranians in the 1980s for carrying out terrorist attacks and assassinations against public officials, as well as for fighting alongside Saddam Husain during his invasion of Iran.

[128] As mentioned in the previous footnote, MEK became rather infamous among Iranians in the 1980s. However, the author is relating a memory from well before all of that. This is likely why his account of these MEK members is a positive one.

[129] Brucellosis is a bacterial infection transmitted from livestock to humans, usually through the consumption of unpasteurised dairy products.

[130] The Raziyeh Firouz hospital is the first private hospital in Kerman, and has remained (with the same name) to this day. It is located on Motahhari Street, near the Imam Mosque.

[131] 1355 SH.

[132] Kerman's Jameh Mosque, which is around 750 years old, is located near Shohada Square (formerly Moshtaghiyeh Square).

[133] Ayatollah Ali-asghar Salehi Kermani (d. 1980) was a revolutionary preacher, a seminary teacher, and the founder of the Masoumiyeh seminary in

I Feared Nothing

Mosque as well as Mr Haqiqi's Quran classes. The Fatemiyeh *tekiyeh*, which was my permanent hang-out, was in its rightful place, as well. Toward the end of the year, a cleric named Seyyed Reza Kamyab[134] came to Kerman and began holding discussions at the Jameh Mosque. Only a small group of people would attend these sessions, making them rather exclusive. I did not understand much from his speeches, perhaps because he exercised a lot of restraint with his words. He was opposed to the Shah; I could gather that much. I ended up participating in three sessions.

Muharram 1976 was when I experienced my first clash with the police. It was Ashura. In previous years, I would spend Ashura at the Jowpar imamzadeh.[135] That day, I stayed in Kerman and paid a visit to my friend Fath-Ali at the Hotel Kasra. The weather was warm, and both of us were looking at the street below from a window. We noticed that some police officers were standing on the other side of the street. A young girl, with uncovered blonde hair (which in those days was a normal sight), walked past them on the pavement. As she passed by, one of the officers gestured to her in a rude manner. This ugly action of his – on the day of Ashura, no less – made me furious. Paying no mind to any potential consequences, I decided to confront him.

Kerman. His body rests in the shrine of the Lady Fatima Masoumeh 🌸, a revered figure among Shia Muslims.

[134] Hojjatul-islam Seyyed Reza Kamyab (d. 1981) was a cleric from the Mashhad seminary and a comrade of the current leader of the Islamic Republic, Seyyed Ali Khamenei. During the revolution, his impassioned speeches in Mashhad, Kerman, and Yazd rallied the masses to the revolutionary cause. After the revolution, he served one term as MP before being assassinated by the Forqan Group, a terrorist group with anti-clerical sentiments.

[135] Jowpar is a summer town in central Kerman, 25 kilometres from the provincial capital.

I Feared Nothing

The municipal officer (who had made the rude gesture) walked toward his friend, who was a traffic officer. They were standing on the junction by the constabulary. Quickly, Fath-Ali and I descended the steps of the hotel. I was angry enough to the extent that consequences did not matter. The two officers were talking with one another. I approached them quickly. With a few karate strikes, I knocked down the municipal cop. Blood began flowing from his nose.

The traffic cop whistled to alert his comrades. Because we were so close to the constabulary, two of them heard the whistle and began running toward us. I managed to escape, and took refuge in the hotel. I hid myself by laying under a bed. Cops stormed the hotel. They spent nearly two hours searching everywhere, but they never found me. Later, I left the hotel and went home. Hitting the officer filled me with pride. Now, I feared nothing.

In the spring of 1977, I went to the holy city of Mashhad. It was my first pilgrimage there. Our bus reached Mashhad after around twenty hours on the road. I rented a room in a travel lodge near the shrine. After making my pilgrimage, I went in search of a local sport club, when a *zurkhāneh* near the shrine caught my eye. By now, I was quite good at lifting *mil* and *kabbādeh*,[136] and was able to do seventy push-ups. Owing to my sportive lifestyle, my arms and chest were quite muscular.

Inside the club, I saw that some middle-aged and younger men were busy with their exercises. A handsome youth, whom everyone called *Āghā* Seyyed Javad, welcomed me in.

---

[136] The *mil* is a type of weight that is used in the *zurkhāneh*. They are club-shaped, quite large, and extremely heavy. *Kabbādeh* are heavy chains used for endurance training.

I Feared Nothing

Wearing an athletic *long*,[137] I entered the *gowd*.[138] I got permission from the *miyān-dār* to begin, and proceeded to do some push-ups.[139] I worked with the *mil*, and then I lifted some stones. From Seyyed Javad's expression, it became clear that I had gained his attention. After finishing my workout, I left the *gowd*; again, with the *miyān-dār*'s permission.

I learned the etiquettes of entering and leaving the *gowd*, which is the peak of a sportsman's etiquette, from the departed Mr Ataei and Haj Mashallah Jahani. In general, sport had a considerable effect on my religious disposition, and was one of the major factors in preventing me from going down a path of moral corruption when I was young. This was especially the case with the ancient sport, whose basis and principles are explicitly moral and religious.[140]

Seyyed Javad, who was from Mashhad himself, asked me where I was from. When I answered that I am from Kerman, he asked for my name, which I gave him. He asked: 'How long will you be in Mashhad for?' I said: 'One week.' He insisted that, for this one week, I go to their club every afternoon.

The shrine of Imam Reza[141] had an indescribable allure. I would stay at the shrine well into the night. The next day, at four o'clock in the afternoon, I went to the club. This time,

---

[137] A *long* is a cloth that covers one's lower body, traditionally worn by athletes within the *zurkhāneh*.
[138] The *gowd* (circle) is the main area of the *zurkhāneh*, wherein the athletes engage in their exercises. The *gowd* is always at a lower level than everywhere else, so as to preserve the humility of the sportsmen.
[139] The *miyān-dār* is the most experienced sportsman in the *zurkhāneh*; the one who has mastery over all the techniques and forms of the ancient sport. He stands in the middle of the *gowd* and directs the group exercises.
[140] The ancient sport, much like East Asian martial arts, has its own peculiar set of etiquettes and rituals. It is thought that, through these etiquettes and rituals, one's soul becomes purified.
[141] Imam Ali ibn Musa al-Ridha.

I Feared Nothing

in addition to Seyyed Javad, there was a young man named Hasan. After the training session, Seyyed Javad and Hasan took me to a corner. From afar it may have appeared as though they wanted to attack someone, but in fact, they wanted to make a pact of friendship with me.

Their build was not an athletic build. Nonetheless, they would do *mil* work, as well as push-ups. However, it was clear that Hasan was rather green, as he would lay listless on the *takhteh* after performing twenty push-ups.[142]

The three of us sat on a gym bench. Seyyed Javad asked: 'Have you ever heard the name Dr Ali Shariati?'[143] I said: 'No, who is that?' The Seyyed, unlike Haj Mohammad, began explaining without any apprehension: 'Shariati is a teacher, and has written some books. He is opposed to the Shah.' Hearing that someone was 'opposed to the Shah' was no longer strange to me. I suppose Seyyed Javad felt I would be receptive to the message.

Then his friend Hasan began speaking, asking me: 'Do you know of Ayatollah Khomeini?'
'No,' I answered.
'Who are you a *muqalid* of?'[144]
'What is a *muqalid*?'

The two of them looked at each other, before deciding not to probe any further about this. Once again, they asked: 'Have you ever even heard the name Khomeini?' I said no. Seyyed and his friend then proceeded to give me a thorough description of the man whom they referred to as Ayatollah Khomeini.

---

[142] The *takhteh* is the wooden plank the athletes hold onto as they perform the push-ups.

[143] Ali Shariati (d. 1977), a prominent intellectual who galvanised many people toward revolutionary struggle in an Islamic context. He is considered to be one of the most influential figures in the Islamic Revolution in Iran.

[144] *Taqlid* is the practice of observing the religious edicts of senior *ulamā* (clergy). The person who does *taqlid* is called a *muqalid*.

I Feared Nothing

Seyyed Javad then checked his surroundings carefully before taking a picture out from under his shirt. He showed me the picture. It was of a bespectacled, middle-aged cleric who was busy studying. At the bottom of the photo, it was written: 'Grand Ayatollah Seyyed Ruhollah Khomeini.'[145] He asked me: 'Do you want me to give you this picture?' Without hesitation, I accepted. Hasan warned me that I mustn't let anyone see the picture, or else I could be arrested by SAVAK (which, by now, I was very much familiar with).

I accepted the picture, hid it beneath my shirt, and said my goodbyes to my new friends. I learned two new names that day: 'Shariati' and 'Khomeini'. I began to ask myself why those ceramic workers from Tehran, with whom I had worked for six whole months and had become close friends, never made any mention of either of these names; even though they spoke so much against the Shah.

I entered the travel lodge and took the picture out from under my shirt. I gazed upon it for hours. I did not go to the gym after that. On the fourth day of my stay, I went to the bus terminal and got a return ticket to Kerman, all while secretly carrying with me this black and white photo, which I now treasured. I felt that I had in my position an object of considerable value.

Upon arriving in Kerman, I showed the picture to Ali Yazdan-panah. Surprised, he said: 'A picture of Mr Khomeini?' He then asked me where I got it from, and warned me: 'If they see you with this picture, they will give you a lot of trouble, or even kill you!" I felt a strange sense of eagerness and bravery within myself. I fancied my karate techniques as a worthy foe to SAVAK; thinking I could quickly knock them all down! My

---

[145] Grand Ayatollah (*āyatullah al-uzmā*) is a title given to the most senior clerics; those who have become *marja'-e taqlid* (reference point for *taqlid*).

I Feared Nothing

entire being was so full of youthful virility that I feared nothing. Now I fancied myself a proper revolutionary; more radical than Ali Yazdan-panah, I spoke openly and without any apprehensions.

By 1977, we began hearing some rumblings about events outside of Kerman. We were, more or less, informed about all the clashes in Qom and Tabriz.[146] In mid-1977, some of the political prisoners of Kerman were freed; among them Mr Hojjati,[147] as well as the Mosharzadeh brothers, one of whom was among the central members of MEK.[148]

Kerman's situation was quickly changing. In the rather quaint city of Kerman, one could now hear the cries of anti-Shah protestors daily. Now, all six of us boys – Ahmad, Ali, myself, Bahram, Sohrab, and Mahmoud – were revolutionists, supporters of Khomeini, and anti-Shah.

Because of my lack of life experience, my youthful virility, and the tribal chivalry which was inherent within us, I would speak ill of the Shah and his family without any reservations. At nights, we – myself, a brother named Vaezi (who would later join the IRGC; I am not sure what became of him after that), Ahmad, and some others – would paint political slogans all across town. Typically, the slogan would be 'Down with the Shah' or 'Long live Khomeini.' The picture of Khomeini was my daily mirror; I would gaze at his picture multiple times throughout the day. It was as if he was sitting right there next to me, reciting the Quran. He became part and parcel of my existence.

---

[146] By that time, protests against the Pahlavi monarchy were intensifying all across Iran.

[147] Hojjatul-islam Mohammad Javad Hojjati Kermani, the first Friday prayer leader of Kerman following the Islamic revolution.

[148] The brother the author is referring to here is Gholam-Hossein Mosharzadeh. The other brother who was freed was Mohammad-Reza Mosharzadeh, a well-mannered and beloved teacher.

I Feared Nothing

I had been taking the driver's license test for some time, and in early 1978, I finally passed. I had to go to the Traffic Police HQ to pick up my license. There was an officer there named Azari-nasab. He told me: 'Come on in. Your license was signed by Khomeini himself! It is ready for you to take.' I did not take the hint from his verbal barb. He guided me to a room. Two ranked[149] officers entered the room and began using some very serious obscenities.

I was besieged by them; there was no means of escape. As they smacked and kicked me, they said some obscenities too inappropriate for me to repeat. One of them said: 'So, you like to write on walls, do you?' They hit me so much that I eventually fell unconscious. Blood flowed from my nose and face. One of them stood on my stomach with his boots and struck me on my stomach so hard that I felt as though all of my internal organs were destroyed. Despite my being an athlete, and despite all of my harsh training in karate and the *zurkhāneh*, I reached my limits and fell unconscious.

When I came to, the door of the room was closed and I was locked in. Because the Traffic Police HQ was across from the hotel where I once worked, the constabulary knew me very well. They referred to me as 'Haj Mohammad's student'. One of the ranked officers informed Haj Mohammad – as well as Haji Karnama, who ran a spare parts shop and knew me well – of my having been detained.

From inside the room, I was able to hear the voices of Haj Mohammad and Haji Karnama, who were telling the police detective: 'He's just a simple, poor worker. He doesn't know about any of this stuff!' They threw in some barbs as well, saying: 'Suppose he made a foolish blunder; this is simply due to his not

---

[149] In Persian, 'ranked' (*darajeh-dār*) refers to anyone with the rank of lieutenant (*sotvān*) and above.

I Feared Nothing

understanding anything!' Whatever their strategy was, it must have worked. After half a day, without handing me over to SAVAK, the police released me from their custody.

With my body having been beaten to a pulp, they held my hands to help me cross the road.[150] They took me to the hotel; to Haj Mohammad. When there, I was served some *sharbat*.[151] After drinking this, I felt a bit better. Haj Mohammad kissed me. He addressed me by saying 'my son' and said to me very calmly: 'If you get caught up with those lads again, they won't show you any mercy.' He insisted that I go back to living and working at the hotel. I thanked him, left the hotel, and went home.

For three days, I could not move due to the severity of the pain. However, I felt a new energy surging in me. The fear of thrashings and torture withered away. I thought: 'Whatever happens, happens!' This event's effect on me was like that of a tattoo (*khāl-kubi*); like the moles I would make on the back of my hands with a pennyroyal branch when I was a child.[152] With every strike and kick that I absorbed, the name 'Khomeini' became more deeply imprinted in the depths of my existence.

I had an opportunity to visit the village again, with Ahmad. The 1356[153] new year was approaching. I remained in the village for some time. Although I had a week off from work at the water company, I didn't feel like going back to work. I ended up staying for ten days.

---

[150] By 'they', the author is likely referring to Haj Mohammad and Haji Karnama.
[151] *Sharbat* is a type of sweet, cold drink consumed in Iran and in some neighbouring countries. It is made from the extracts of flower petals or fruits.
[152] While *khāl-kubi* is now used to refer to tattoos as a whole, historically it referred to a specific type of tattoo wherein one imprints a mole (*khāl*) upon their skin.
[153] The start of 1356 SH coincides with the spring of 1977.

I Feared Nothing

My parents were happy that I was a 'government employee'. Of course, they did not understand very well the distinction between a worker and a functionary. Just the fact that I was among the handful of people from our small village who were earning wages from the government was a big deal.

However, there was an entirely different commotion going on in my heart. By now, every revolutionist had become familiar with BBC Radio. Every night, I would listen to the BBC along with my older brother, who by now was more zealous than myself in religious matters. While the BBC used much embellishment and hyperbole in reporting the daily events in Tehran and other cities, the Shah's regime was still powerful.

In our age group, almost without exception (aside from a few who were dependent upon the tribal chief), everyone had a sense of revolutionary zeal and were generally sons of the lower class. Our small village was, thus, supporting the revolution in unison. However, my mother and father did not know all the details of our political entanglements.

When I returned to Kerman, I saw that the revolutionary zeal was greater than it once was. For a month, I got back to work. However, I no longer had the impetus to go. With Ahmad and our two younger brothers, we rented a room in a house. It was the four of us in one room; one room which served as our bedroom, storage, kitchen, and everything else.

It was just us and our *ham-shahri*s, who were daily guests at our simple *sofreh* which generally consisted of bread with yoghurt or eggs, or bread with *halvā*.[154] Sometimes, we would serve the foods my mother had given me; *pest*, or sometimes stews or mixed nuts. On the other side of the courtyard of our rental

---

[154] *Halvā*, in the Anglosphere, usually denotes sesame *halvā* (which, in Iran, is called *halvā-ardeh*). However, in Iran, when one says simply *halvā*, they are referring to a different type of *halvā*; one that is made using flour and rosewater. This is what the author is referring to here.

I Feared Nothing

home,[155] there was a family with children – most of whom were young girls – renting another room. At lunch time, those children would share in our bread and yoghurt feast. Generously, we – and of course, Ahmad more so than myself – would crumble the bread inside the yoghurt bowl and feed them. Sometimes, we would not even get full ourselves, while the kids were completely stuffed with yoghurt. Their mother would come by and pray for our well-being, as thanks for feeding her children.

By now, I was spending more time in the Jameh Mosque than the Fatemiyeh *tekiyeh*. In fact, the Jameh Mosque is where I spent most of my days. And of course, I never neglected to go to the sporting club; mostly to Haj Mashallah's Jahan Club. I also found new friends: Ata and Haj Abbas Zangi-abadi.[156] When Haj Abbas lifted stones, his robust physique would draw everyone's attention. Sometimes, I would also stop by Ata's club. Ata, who owned this club, was also considered to be among the *pahlevān*s of Kerman.[157] Because of my respect for elders and for the sport, both Haj Mashallah and Ataei respected me.

Protests in the cities began to gain steam. Familiarity with the Imam ﷺ was no longer limited to only a handful of people.[158] Droves of people now knew him and awaited his return.[159] Kerman was so full of revolutionaries that one might say it played a central role in the revolution. Hashemi Rafsanjani

---

[155] Traditional homes in Kerman (and many other Iranian cities) are designed such that there are multiple rooms connected to a shared courtyard, which usually has a shallow pool of water (*howz*) for washing and cleaning.
[156] By Ata, the author is referring to the aforementioned Mr Ataei.
[157] A *pahlevān* is a champion of the ancient sport, although in colloquial use it may also be used to describe weightlifters or amateur wrestlers. The author is using the more specific meaning here.
[158] The author is referring to the aforementioned Ayatollah Khomeini, who by now was called 'Imam' by his supporters.
[159] Khomeini spent many years in exile before returning to Iran following the Shah's abdication.

I Feared Nothing

(whom I did not know of at the time),[160] Bahonar, Hojjati, Fahim Kermani,[161] the Mosharzadeh brothers, the Movahedis,[162] Saveh,[163] Jafari,[164] and the majority of the *ulamā* of Kerman (apart from a few individuals), were all united in being opposed to the Shah.

The Jameh Mosque and Malek Mosque were now the main areas where revolutionaries would congregate. Prior to that, this was the role of the Qa'em Mosque; in large part due to the presence of Ayatollah Haqiqi. But now, because of the leadership and central role of Ayatollah Salehi, the Jameh Mosque became the main axis of revolutionary activity. Salehi was an elderly, short, and enlightened man who was intensely respected and known by most people in Kerman.

Everyone would congregate in the afternoons. News was spread through unofficial means. Everyone had some news from here and there – from Tehran, to Qom, to Shiraz – and would pass the news on to one another.

For the first time in Kerman, the clergy were now at the front lines of the protests. Ayatollah Najafi, who led prayer in the Imam Zaman Mosque, was the vanguard. The rest of the clergy were marching along with him, with the people in tow. The initial slogans were about political prisoners and demanding their freedom, but gradually the slogans began taking on an anti-Shah

---

[160] Akbar Hashemi Rafsanjani (d. 2017) was a revolutionary cleric who would go on to become the president of Iran from 1989 to 1997.

[161] Morteza Fahim-Kermani (b. 1932) was a revolutionary cleric who, after the revolution, became an MP representing Kerman province.

[162] The author refers to 'the Movahedis' (in the plural). One of them is almost certainly Ayatollah Mohammad-Ali Movahedi-Kermani (b. 1931), who is currently among the leaders of Friday prayers in Tehran.

[163] Likely referring to Abdolhossein Saveh (d. 2000), who after the revolution became an MP representing Kerman province.

[164] Seyyed Yahya Jafari (d. 2020), a revolutionary cleric who would go on to become the leader of Friday prayers in Kerman.

tinge. Like a small flame growing into a firestorm, eventually the cries of 'Down with the Shah' echoed throughout the city.

All the security forces were thrown into action: the military police, the constabulary, SAVAK... and even the army, deployed from the 05 Training Garrison (which I had visited during my brother's army days).[165] However, the wave of masses was far larger than their capacity to stop it. Arresting one or two, or even a thousand people, would not be sufficient to stop this wave. Indeed, it was impossible for such an insignificant number of arrests to have an effect.

Me and my friends – a group which now included Alijan and Abdollah, as well – spoke our minds without a care in the world. One morning, it was announced that there would be a protest at the Jameh Mosque. This announcement was spread, by word of mouth, even faster than it could have been by the social media of today. As a result, the whole city turned up!

Young revolutionaries, along with some members of the clergy (among them Ayatollah Salehi), gathered in the *shabestān*.[166] The municipal police recruited some Gypsies who were living in the periphery of the city to help them converge on the mosque from both flanks. The Jameh Mosque had three rather large entrances; similar in size to one another.

I had just purchased a yellow Suzuki 125 motorcycle. I entered the *qadam-gāh*[167] door – which faced the Kerman bazaar – and parked the motorcycle in a side alley which branched off from the bazaar. There was much commotion within the mosque.

---

[165] This garrison has since been renamed the Shahid General Alireza Ashraf Ganjavi Training Garrison.

[166] A *shabestān* is an underground space commonly found in traditional Iranian architecture (to include Iranian mosques); usually used in the summers as a refuge from the heat.

[167] A *qadam-gāh* is a place where it is believed that a saint or holy personage has stepped before.

I Feared Nothing

After some hours of tension, the Gypsies – with the support of the constabulary – began their onslaught; attacking from the mosque's northern and western doors. First, they set fire to every motorcycle and set of wheels that was parked in front of the mosque door. The youths cried out for the doors of the mosque to be closed.

I went to the roof of the *shabestān* along with Vaezi and Ahmad. The Gypsies and police forces were aggressively burning people's vehicles. They approached the mosque door with motorcycles and lit the door on fire. Then, they began firing tear gas into the mosque from both flanks. The doors were now opened, and thus they began their onslaught on the *shabestān*.

I evacuated Ayatollah Salehi from the *shabestān*. He had gone unconscious due to his old age and inhaling so much gas. A non-conformist cleric named Asadi – who I would later become friends with – was passionately rallying the youths in their confrontation with the police. People attempted to flee through the western door, but whoever escaped through this door would be on the receiving end of some broken bones, courtesy of the Gypsies' bludgeons and clubs.

In the heat of the battle, I saw a child who was frightened and crying. Reflexively, I confronted the cop who was attacking him. I said: 'Let him go!' I said these words so harshly that it seemed, for a moment, he became hesitant and scared. I grabbed the child and exited the mosque through the western door. Then, I circled around and went toward the *qadam-gāh*. My motorbike was fine. Ahmad and I mounted the bike and took off, when suddenly a flock of cops appeared before us. We took many blows to the head from their batons before managing to get through them.

I Feared Nothing

The clash had spilled over into Mohammad Reza Shah Street.[168] We attacked the police by throwing stones at them. The police set the Oghabi brothers' shop (which sold motorcycles and bicycles) ablaze. The Oghabis – although they were among the wealthy property-owners of Kerman – were opposed to the Shah. The clash extended well into the night, but ultimately the protest was broken up.

Two days later, we – myself, Vaezi, and Fath-Ali, as well as some other youths from the city – burned down the only liquor store in the city, which was on Kazemi Street.[169] The forces affiliated with the regime had lost all recourses. The news of their having set fire to Kerman's Jameh Mosque circulated throughout the country and was the catalyst for various protests. In Kerman itself, some very large protests would follow. Their slogan: 'Kerman's mosque, the Quran, the Muslim people: the Shah set them all ablaze.'

I was always hanging around the Jameh Mosque. I do not remember when I would even manage to eat lunch and dinner. I stopped going to the water company. I was on strike, so I refrained from going to work. In the mosque, some of the lads came up with some slogans: 'We will not live under the yoke of tyranny. We will sacrifice our lives on the path of liberation. We will upend this Pahlavi dynasty.' 'Down with the Shah, down with the Shah.' 'O Shah, the traitor, you will become a wanderer; you have destroyed the soil of the motherland.'[170]

---

[168] This street is now named Taleghani Street, after the revolutionary cleric Ayatollah Seyyed Mahmoud Taleghani (d. 1979).

[169] This street has since been renamed Qods Steet.

[170] In their original Persian, these slogans rhyme:
'*Zir-e bār-e setam nemikonim zendegi; jān fadā mikonim dar rah-e āzādegi; zir o ru mikonim selseleh-ye pahlavi.*'
'*Marg bar shāh; marg bar shāh.*'
'*Ey shāh-e khā'en, āvāreh gardi; khāk-e vatan ra virāneh kardi.*'

I Feared Nothing

Even in our village, my family, Mash Aziz, and Ahmad's father had all become anti-Shah. My older brother would listen to the BBC every night for news. On the day of Ashura in 1978,[171] the Rabor gendarmerie – along with the tribal chief – assembled outside our home with drums and musical instruments, chanting 'Long live the Shah.'[172] In doing this, they were sending a message to my father: 'Watch your back.' My older brother Hossein was distraught, and shocked that they would do this on the day of Ashura. He kept repeating: 'I can't believe they did this on the day of Ashura,' affixed his eyes to the ground, and cried. Everyone thought that he had gone mad.

I returned to our village once again. My brother's state made me worried. I spent three days with him, and told him the news from the cities; about the revolution, and about how the Shah was close to being overthrown. I would take him outside and talk to him continuously. On the third day, he returned to his normal mood. I recommended that he stop listening to the BBC for awhile.

Once I was back in Kerman, my mother became worried and came to pay me a visit. She was worried that my younger brother would be killed. She made me swear that I not get involved in confrontations with the authorities. Coincidentally, while my mother was in the city, the revolution was reaching its zenith. It was around this time that Ahmad Tavakoli was martyred.[173]

I began searching for a weapon. First, I bought a dummy weapon, but it was of no use. Then, I thought to take the armament of a police officer who was a friend of a friend. I had

---

[171] 1357 SH.

[172] The slogan *jāvid shāh* literally translates to 'May the Shah live forever.'

[173] The author has likely made a transcription error here in writing 'Ahmad'. This person's name was likely Hasan Tavakoli, of whose burial the author alludes to in the coming paragraphs.

seen him some time ago and saw that he had a Colt M-1911 pistol at his waist. I felt that I could take him. Due to being sportive, as well as the pridefulness of youth and the impetuousness which the revolution had given us, I had absolutely zero fear of confronting the police. With my friend Fath-Ali, we devised a plan: we were to invite him to the hotel, knock him out unconscious with a strike to the head, and take his weapon. However, this plan was never implemented.

Three months later, someone brought me a Colt (with the monarchy's coat of arms engraved on it) from Ravar.[174] It cost five thousand tomans.[175] There was no need for any training. It looked just like the dummy Colt that I already had.

After the burial of Hasan Tavakoli, we performed his funeral ceremony in the Malek Mosque (which today is called the Imam Khomeini Mosque). Many people attended. Police forces, along with many people from the periphery of Kerman who were said to be from Baghin,[176] made a show of force in the street and seemed to be making their way the mosque. I alerted the mosque.

As their column was approaching the mosque, a lorrie carrying bricks caught my eye. With my friend Hasan, we attacked the police forces with bricks. Our confrontation began before they reached the mosque, but they entered. First, they fired blanks. Later, they began firing live rounds. When they fired, everyone shouted: 'They're firing blanks!' But little by little, the live rounds came to the fore. Moments later, three people fell to the ground: Shahid Dadbin, Shahid Namjoo, and others, who were martyred then and there. Until one o'clock in the morning, we proceeded to clash with the police in the streets and alleyways surrounding the mosque.

---

[174] Ravar is the northernmost town of Kerman province, and lies 140 kilometres from the provincial capital.
[175] At the time, this was worth roughly 715 US dollars.
[176] Baghin is a town in the periphery of Kerman city.

Figure 1: Young Qasem

I Feared Nothing

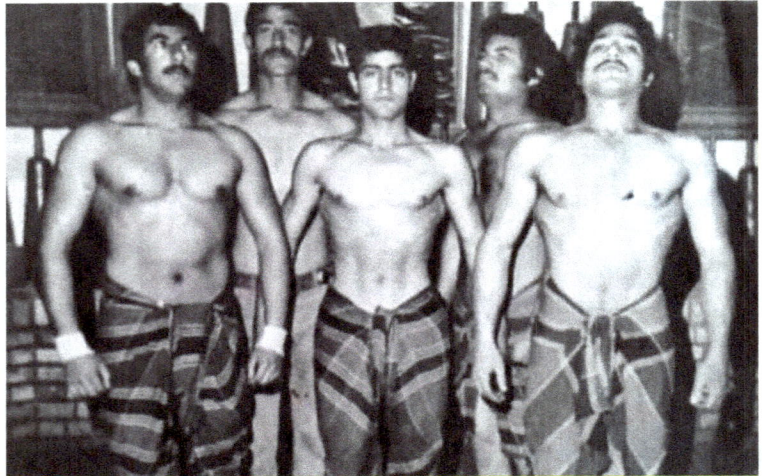

Figure 2: Qasem (centre) and his mates at the zurkhāneh

Figure 3: Division commander Soleimani gets some R&R during the 'Imposed War'

Figure 4: Another picture from the 'Imposed War' times. Soleimani (far left) commanded the IRGC's 41st 'Tharallah' Infantry Division during this conflict.

Figure 5: General Soleimani in Aleppo during the decisive battle (2012-2016) of the Syrian conflict

Figure 6: General Soleimani reciting Quran

Figure 7: General Soleimani at a meeting of IRGC commanders

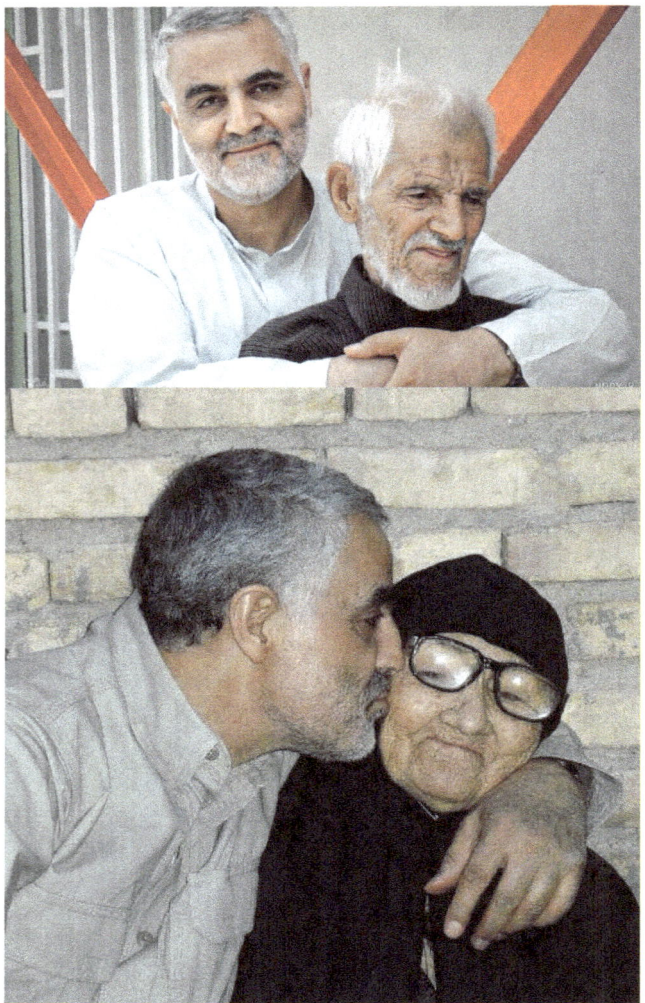
Figure 8: Soleimani always retained a special fondness for his parents

Figure 9: Funeral procession for General Soleimani, his Iraqi comrade Abu Mahdi al-Muhandis, and the others killed in the assassination (Najaf, Iraq)

Figure 10: General Soleimani's children at his burial in Kerman

I Feared Nothing

Figure 11: A mural in Tehran's Vali-e Asr Square (some time in 2020), depicting Soleimani and Abu Mahdi in the courtyard of Imam Husain's ﷺ shrine in Karbala. The text reads: 'Send our salutations. While we may be estranged, we speak in remembrance of you.'

www.ingramcontent.com/pod-product-compliance
Lightning Source LLC
Chambersburg PA
CBHW072106110526
44590CB00018B/3330